> *Until America comes to terms with the condition and unresolved issues of American Indians, questions will continue to haunt the nation's conscience.*
> *If the Indians lose…we all lose.*

THUNDERBIRD ENTERPRISES
American Indian Marketing & Data Resources
8821 N. 1st Street • Phoenix, AZ • 85020-2801

This is the 3rd annual edition of the American Indian Digest. Each edition will contain a core of current demographics, but Indian issues and related thinking will change. Demographics will be generated in the foreseeable future by computer networks.

"The Transition" is a pencil drawing by Indian artist Lyle James. Lyle James was born in Kalkaska, Michigan and is a member of the Ottawa Tribe. He is a multi-talented artist who works in pencil, pen, and charcoal pastels as well as watercolors and acrylic paintings. One of Lyle's particular talents is the ability to artistically transfer the face from a photograph to an Indian portrayal.

Lyle is internationally known for his artwork. People who have acquired his work are President Carter, Bob Hope, Phyllis Diller, Senator Jackie Vaughn, and Pat Paulson. He has paintings on display at Michigan State University, in the Voyage Room at the Kellog Center.

Lyle James can be contacted by calling Thunderbird Enterprises.

➤ TABLE OF CONTENTS

➤ FOREWORD

MISSION STATEMENT

The Digest has two primary purposes. First, to change the public perception of American Indians by the presentation of historical synopsis from an Indian perspective, and then focus on contemporary demographics. Secondly, to be instrumental in the Indian political unification process by presenting a national perspective with regard to people and resources.

The demographic data can be utilized as a basis to make projections if a certain course of action is taken or continued. Hopefully, the conclusions will be a catalyst to initiate dialogue with regard to the long-term future of the Indian people.

The primary function of the Digest is to be a convenient source of basic Indian information and a reference source for additional information. The bibliography lists the addresses and telephone numbers for major reference sources.

The Digest is not meant to be a study in Indian anthropology. The subject of Indians is so vast, complex and diverse, that it would take a lifetime of study to begin to understand the people and their problems.

Whenever Indians are mentioned, the image is almost always within a historical or cultural context. These areas of interest are very important and have been cultivated extensively, while contemporary information has essentially been excluded.

Today, in the continental United States; there are 2 million Indians - affiliated with 319 tribes - living on 308 reservations. Each of these issues is much more complex than they appear. The Digest offers an insight into these issues.

Libraries, universities and museums contain voluminous resources that chronicle every aspect of the fascinating epic as two conflicting cultures engaged in a violent and savage struggle for survival. For American Indians the struggle continues.

Global Perspective

Carl Sagan and space shuttles have let us peek into the foreseeable future as scientists systematically explore and analyze the galaxy. What they find will affect the life of every person on this planet. Space programs are already busy designing space stations. Are other planets inhabitable? Is there intelligent life on these planets? What effect will these answers have on our religious beliefs?

The launching pads of space exploration are the foundation for a quantum leap in global perception and evolution. We know that the earth looks like a giant blue and white marble suspended in space. The moon has changed from a globe of romantic mystique to dusty volcanos and static human voices. The stars have changed from twinkling points of light to satellites ringed by planes of dust and matter.

Cost-effective telecommunications have transformed the world into a global community that is a global market. Competitive participation is mandatory in the global market for national economic survival. International business is conducted across oceans as easily as between states.

An indicator of the imminence of the global market is the implementation of the metric system in the United States. The United States has been flirting with the metric system for the last 20 years. Now it is mandated by specifications for participation in government contracts.

The role of American Indians in the marketplace

"International daily business is now conducted across oceans as easily as between states."

has traditionally been as a local source of arts and crafts products. Indian arts and crafts are a multi-billion dollar business with domestic and global markets. The time has come for Indians to make the transition from supplier to entrepreneur in these markets.

RACIAL PREJUDICE

As man adapted to his geographic environment, he developed certain physical characteristics, learned to walk upright, lost some body hair, and became a social creature. Tribal prejudice became a human instinct based on fear and was necessary for survival. Most human beings still have some degree of tribal prejudice. People are most comfortable around people like themselves.

Racial prejudice is a mutation of tribal prejudice that evolved from fear to hate. When carried to the extreme, racial prejudice festers into racism. Racism is learned and is generational. If the older folks would leave the kids alone, it will dissipate very rapidly.

Racism is socially archaic, maliciously ignorant, and non-productive. It becomes an insidious emotional cancer that leaves the carrier mentally stunted. Mental evolution has simply not kept pace with physical evolution.

In today's society, human similarities are more important than racial differences. Within the next 2 generations, racism as we know it will be a moot issue. It's a waste of time on a foregone conclusion.

The ideals of democracy are a tribute to man's conceptual humanity. Only human nature stands in the way. It is neither rational nor moral for those who enjoy the tenets of democracy, to deny the same basic rights to others because of their difference in appearance or ideology.

An American paradox: on one hand, racial diversity is one source of the nation's strength; and on the other, it's the source of one of its severest social problems. Like

"We hold these truths to be self-evident, that all men are created equal, that they are endowed by their Creator with certain unalienable Rights, that among these are Life, Liberty and the pursuit of Happiness."

Declaration of Independence - 1776

it or not, racial diversity is an inherent component of American society, and America is an inherent component of a global community.

Through modern technology, we are about to discover that historically racial blood mixing was more prevalent and extensive than we have realized. American minorities are currently out-marrying at a rate of over 50%.

The face of the majority of Americans will be shades of brown by 2050. And so each race will come to terms with it's vested interest in other races and lay the issue to rest.

America must resolve the issues of domestic racism before undertaking the problems of a multi-cultural global market. There are six billion people in the world. America is only 5% of the world market and cannot afford racism.

When the course of human development is viewed from a telescopic galaxy perspective, racism becomes insignificant. Americans will have more pressing matters to deal with than the blood composition or the skin pigmentation of their neighbors.

Indians must be conscious and wary of practicing insidious racism. Dissension and prejudice permeate nearly every aspect of Indian life. This is the same racism that Indians have endured for hundreds of years. The same racism that nearly exterminated the Indian people. The same racism that has kept Indians divided, vulnerable and manageable.

"Peace comes within the souls of men when they realize their relationship, their oneness, with the universe and all its powers, and realize that the center is really everywhere. It is within each of us."

Black Elk

➤ CHAPTER 1 • Historical Synopsis

Chronology

This abbreviated roster of historical events, significantly influenced the course of Indian destiny and provides a chronological perspective.

1492	Arrival of Columbus to the New World.
1607	Jamestown was founded.
1620	Pilgrims land at Plymouth Rock.
1622	First major Indian retaliation.
1744	The Treaty of Lancaster.
1775	American Revolutionary War begins.
1776	US Declaration of Independence.
1778	First treaty between US & Indians.
1783	American Revolutionary War ends.
1803	US Louisiana purchase for $15 million.
1824	BIA established under Dept. of War.
1830	Indian Removal Act.
1848	First gold strike in the West.
1850	U.S. eliminates all foreign land claims.
1854	Indian Appropriation Act.
1861	Civil War begins.
1862	Railroad Act.
1865	Civil War ends.
1868	Fort Laramie peace conference.
1871	Treaties end between US & Indians.
1887	General Allotment Act. (Dawes Act)
1917	U.S. enters World War I.
1919	Treaty of Versailles ends World War II.
1924	Indian Citizenship Act.
1941	U.S. enter World War II.
1944	National Congress of American Indians.
1945	World War II ends with the atomic bomb.
1947	Indian Claims Commission Act.
1948	Indians allowed to vote in Arizona.

1953 Liquor Prohibition repealed for Indians.
1962 Indians allowed to vote in New Mexico.
1968 Indian Civil Rights Act.
1972 Indian Education Act.
1975 Indian Self-Determination Act.
1978 American Indian Religious Freedom Act.
1988 Indian Gaming Regulatory Act.

Myth & Misconception

There is considerable speculation with regard to the origin and time-line of the arrival of American Indians to the continent. Technology is providing the means for scientific discovery which indicates that Indian history may be much older than has been generally accepted. Indians also have their own versions of origin and time.

The prevalent theory is that, at least 12,000 years ago, Indian ancestors crossed the frozen Bering Straits, fanned out from Alaska and established civilizations on two continents.

1492

From the arrival of Columbus to the present, the truth about Indians has been obscured by myth and misconception. Columbus accidently landed in the Caribbean Islands while seeking a new trade route to the Far East. The truth is that Columbus never set foot on the continent we know as America and yet he was historically given recognition for "discovering" America.

First - Columbus was not the first to explore the new world. An interesting book titled: "Columbus Was Last" by Patrick Hughey, offers the compelling premise

> **"They are artless and generous with what they have... With 50 men we could subjugate them all and make them do whatever we want."**
>
> **Columbus - 1493**

that there were 15-20 substantial foreign contacts prior to the arrival of Columbus.

Secondly - Aztec, Mayan, Mound Builders, Pueblos and other existing Indian civilizations were comparable, and in some respects superior, to the contemporary civilizations of Europe.

Regardless of the circumstances, the arrival of Columbus was a historical accomplishment of the first magnitude which initiated a chain of events that changed the world forever.

Columbus was convinced that he had landed in India and called the native inhabitants "Indians." The "Indian" misnomer has been accepted to the extent that it is synonymous with all indigenous people in the western hemisphere.

America's native people have been known as -

- "Indians" for 450 years;

- "American Indians" since World War II;

- "Native Americans" for the last 20 years;

- "First Americans", "First Nations" and a host of other names are under consideration.

For our purposes, we will use *American Indian* and *Indian* designations interchangeably and leave the politically correct semantics to the academic community and future generations.

AMERICA'S HOLOCAUST

Most American Indians view the arrival of Columbus as the beginning of a 400 year cycle of diseases, exploitation, enslavement and genocide that devastated them as a race of people. In 400 years, the massive number of Indians essentially exterminated by the attrition of genocide is speculative. The ramifications of

> **"Before we can set out on the road to success, we have to know where we are going, and before we can know that we must determine where we have been in the past."**
>
> John F. Kennedy - 1963

those sustained extermination policies exist today as shortened life expectancy due to emotional and health problems.

After initial fears had subsided, most Indians were curious and even friendly toward the strange invaders. A touch of irony, some eastern tribes helped settlers survive the first critical winters. However, conflict between settlers and Indians was inevitable because the Indian value system was simply not compatible with that of the settlers.

Many Indians tribes had developed nomadic lifestyles that were in harmony with the seasons and environment. Their lifestyles were in direct conflict with the fixed homesteads, farms and industrial activity of the European settlers.

The concept of individual land ownership was alien to Indians. Indians believed the elements of the environment were inseparable and could not be owned by individuals. Their high regard for the environment was reflected by the inclusion of the elements in most religious ceremonies. The concept of Mother Earth and some special features of the land such as mountains are considered sacred. The issue was compounded by the idea that land ownership could be transferred by a piece of paper.

Settlers considered Indians indolent and felt they did not make good use of the land, therefore, they should yield to people who would use the land for more productive purposes. The settlers rationalized that Indians had no moral right to obstruct the expansion of a higher civilization. Settlers adopted a doctrine of *"manifest destiny by divine providence"* as they moved steadily Westward.

For over 100 years, European nations made sporadic attempts to establish settlements along the Eastern seaboard. The first permanent settlement was Jamestown, an English colony established in 1607. The

Pilgrims landed at Plymouth Rock in 1620. As other colonies were established, settlers began an aggressive policy of expansion by attrition.

Indians resisted with open hostility. The first major retaliation occurred in 1622, when Powhatan leader Opechancanough went on a rampage in Virginia and killed 347 settlers. The conflict initiated a pattern of reciprocal atrocities that lasted for nearly 300 years.

By the time the settlers were entrenched along the eastern seaboard, resentment and antagonism toward Indians had escalated. They were considered a sub-human race that must be removed or exterminated. The prevalent attitude tolerated and encouraged the practice of genocide and slavery.

During this same period of time, Spanish encroachment was taking place along the West coast and in the Southwest.

Indians were brutalized and killed with impunity because they did not have a basis for legal recognition or recourse in the country. A case in point: In the early 1800s, there were an estimated 260,000 Indians in California, by 1900, there were 20,000. Indians could not bear witness against a white man in a court of law. Indians were categorically granted citizenship by the magnanimous Indian Citizenship Act in 1924.

Many colonies, states and territories paid bounties for Indian extermination. Bounties varied from $25 to $130 for each male scalp and usually half of that amount for women and children. *The only good Indian is a dead Indian"* and *"nits become lice"* were typical expressions that reflected attitudes that lasted for 400 years.

The 1744 Treaty of Lancaster established the Appalachian Mountains as the physical boundary between the settlers and Indians. This general boundary was reaffirmed geographically when the 13 Colonies won

By 1671, there were 50,000 settlers in the Colonies.

"The ramifications of those sustained extermination policies exist today as shortened life expectancy due to emotional and health problems."

their war for independence and became the United
States of America.

As settler's numbers multiplied, their insatiable
demand for land forced Indians westward as they

By His EXCELLENCY

WILLIAM SHIRLEY, Esq;

Captain-General and Governor in Chief, in and over His Majesty's Province of the *Massachusetts-Bay*, in *New-England*, and Vice-Admiral of the same, and Major-General in His Majesty's Army.

A PROCLAMATION.

HEREAS the Indians of *Norridgewock, Arresagunaook, Weweenock* and *St. John's* Tribes, and the Indians of the other Tribes inhabiting in the Eastern and Northern Parts of His Majesty's Territories of *New-England*, the *Penobscot* Tribe only excepted, have, contrary to their solemn Submission unto His Majesty long since made and frequently renewed, been guilty of the most perfidious, barbarous and inhuman Murders of divers of his Majesty's *English* Subjects; and have abstained from all Commerce and Correspondence with His Majesty's said Subjects for many Months past; and the said *Indians* have fully discovered an inimical, traiterous and rebellious Intention and Disposition;

I have therefore thought fit to issue this Proclamation, and to Declare the Indians of the Norridgewock, Arresaguntacook, Weweenock and St. John's Tribes, and the Indians of the other Tribes new or late inhabiting in the Eastern and Northern Parts of His Majesty's Territories of New-England, and in Alliance and Confederacy with the above-recited Tribes, the Penobscots only excepted, to be Enemies, Rebels and Traitors to his most Sacred Majesty: And I do hereby require His Majesty's Subjects of this Province to embrace all Opportunities of pursuing, captivating, killing and destroying all and any of the aforesaid Indians, the Penobscots excepted.

AND WHEREAS the General Court of this Province have voted, That a Bounty or Encouragement be granted and allowed to be paid out of the Publick-Treasury to the marching Army that shall be employed for the Defence of the Eastern and Western Frontiers from the Twenty-fifth of this Month of *June* until the Twenty-fifth of *November* next;

I have thought fit to publish the same; and I do hereby promise, That there shall be paid out of the Province-Treasury to all and any of the said Forces, over and above their Bounty upon Enlistment, their Wages and Subsistence, the Premiums or Bounties following, viz.

For every Male Indian Prisoner above the Age of Twelve Years, that shall be taken and brought to *Boston, Fifty Pounds.*

For every Male Indian Scalp, brought in as Evidence of their being killed, *Forty Pounds.*

For every Female Indian Prisoner, taken and brought in as aforesaid, and for every Male Indian Prisoner under the Age of Twelve Years, taken and brought in as aforesaid, *Twenty-five Pounds.*

For every Scalp of such Female Indian or Male Indian under Twelve Years of Age, brought in Evidence of their being killed, as aforesaid, *Twenty Pounds.*

GIVEN under my Hand at Boston, in the Province aforesaid, this Twelfth Day of June, 1755, and in the Twenty-eighth Year of the Reign of our Sovereign Lord GEORGE the Second, by the Grace of GOD, of Great-Britain, France, and Ireland, KING, Defender of the Faith, &c.

By His Excellency's Command,
J. WILLARD, *Sec'y.*

Courtesy Pioneer Historical Society

W. Shirley.

GOD Save the KING.

BOSTON, Printed by *John Draper*, Printer to His ' the Honourable His Majesty's COUNCIL. 1755.

*In 1755, the British crown offered 40 pounds for Indian male scalps and
20 pounds for females and children.*

1790

By 1790, the population of the United States was 4 million.

By 1829, the population of the United States was 12.5 million.

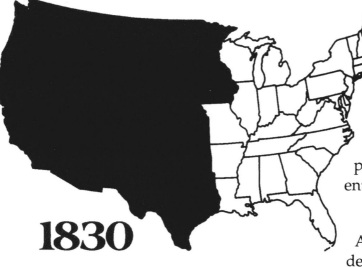

1830

fought a losing battle for territory and survival. The conflicts became a war of bizarre perpetual retaliations. Historical records implicate both sides as participants in macabre atrocities.

Most Indian fatalities were caused by diseases rather than by warfare. Indians had very little immunity to European diseases that were introduced to them as a matter of course, but sometimes by design. Epidemics of smallpox, cholera, malaria, syphilis and influenza are a few of the diseases that decimated the Indian population. Many tribes were essentially wiped out by the thousands. In some instances, the devastation was so complete that pious settlers considered the epidemics as *"divine providence."*

Survivors of disease and genocide were subject to the widespread practice of slavery. Indians were sold as slaves to work plantations and mines. Conquest has been standard operating procedure since man became "civilized" - even among Indians. The victims of conquest suffer "man's inhumanity to man". Indians practiced bondage and other atrocities as rituals of intertribal warfare for centuries. However, the white slave traders escalated the practice to a scale of commercial enterprise.

The 1830 Indian Removal Act, signed into law by President Andrew Jackson, extinguished Indian land rights East of the Mississippi. It provided for their relocation to "Indian Country", which was defined as "the part of the United States West of the Mississippi and not within the states of Missouri, Louisiana or the territory of Arkansas.

This definitive boundary seemed to create a brief pause in the settler's voracious appetite for Indian lands. However, an ominous tidal wave of immigrants was building along the western frontier.

By 1850, the United States had extinguished all European land claims from coast to coast, setting the stage for the settlement of the West. Only the Indians stood in the way of progress.

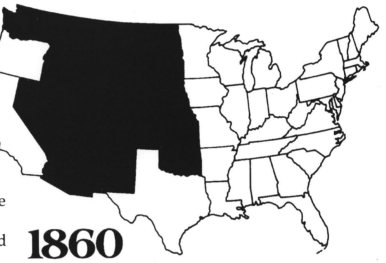

1860

The 1854 Indian Appropriation Act gave Congress the authority to establish Indian Reservations. The act provided the legal basis for removal of specific Indians to specific locations. In 1862, President Lincoln signed the Homestead Act and Railroad Act into law which became major factors in crushing Indian resistance.

By 1860, the population of the United States was 31 million.

The discovery of gold in the West and availability of free land launched a stampede of humanity across the land. When the dust settled, Indian land rights had essentially been extinguished and the devastated Indian had nearly been exterminated. In the wake of this carnage, the western half of a new nation was born.

By 1890, the last of the Indian wars were over and the 1887 Indian Allotment Act was the "coup de grace" for Indian tribal land rights. The essence of this act was to eliminate the rights of Indians to hold tribal land in common. Those rights were exchanged for individual-

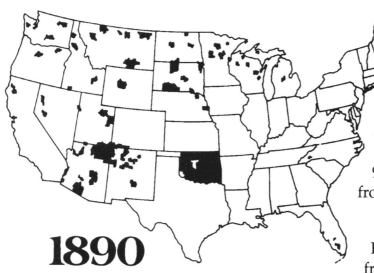

1890

By 1890, the population of the United States was 63 million.

ized allotments of 160 acres per head of household, with lesser acreages to individuals. The surplus land was ceded to the government and sold to the settlers. More than 100 reservations were allotted and over 90 million acres were abstracted from Indian lands.

In less than 100 years, Indian lands had been reduced from all land west of the Appalachian Mountains to desolate reservations totaling less than 4% of the continental United States.

During the development of this country, tremendous hardships were endured by immigrants of all races. There has always been a "pecking order" as each new ethnic group struggled to weave their particular talents into the fabric of America. Equal integration seems to require a more resolute will from some racial groups than others.

American Indians fought for their inalienable aboriginal land rights. The fierce resistance resulted in 400 years of Indian bashing that left a physically deteriorated people with deep psychological wounds. Indians had lost their land, self-image, self-esteem and were rapidly becoming a vanishing race.

Ironically, during intense oppression of Indians, the United States fought the Revolutionary War for freedom and independence. The Emancipation Proclamation, President Lincoln's declaration to free the black race from slavery, was a cornerstone of the Civil War. These lofty ideals were to establish the moral fiber and political creed of the United States.

The rhetorical question is, *"Could the Indian dilemma*

have been resolved in a more humane and equitable manner?"
Probably not within the context of the times.

Groundless Treaties

> *"The utmost good faith shall always be observed toward the Indians; their land and property shall never be taken from them without their consent; and in their property, rights and liberty, they shall never be invaded or disturbed, unless in just and lawful wars authorized by Congress; but laws founded on justice and humanity shall from time to time be made, for preventing wrongs done to them, and for preserving peace and friendship with them."*
>
> **United States Congress**
> **Northwest Ordinance – 1787**

Because Indians were the sole inhabitants of the North American continent, it was imperative for European nations to establish a legal concept of aboriginal land rights as a basis for treaty negotiations. Treaties became the legal basis used by encroaching settlers to appropriate Indian lands.

Typical treaty negotiations were based on huge Indian land cessions in exchange for reservation areas, food, hardware goods and annuity payments. During the translation from document to reality, questionable sincerity succumbed to avarice and self-serving rationalization. The government's "perpetual guaranty" of Indian lands did not endure; and the delivery of food, goods and monies failed to match the promises.

Indians were at a distinct disadvantage during treaty negotiations because the treaty documents were written in a language Indians did not understand. Treaties were interpreted to Indians leaders who rarely knew what was actually written on the document placed before them for mark or signature. Other ruses included negotiation of a treaty with a manageable

"We the people of the United State, in order to form a more perfect Union, establish justice, insure domestic tranquility, provide for the common defense, promote the general welfare, and secure the blessings of liberty to ourselves and our posterity, do ordain and establish this Constitution for the United States of America."

Preamble to the Constitution - 1776

> **"Treaties became the legal basis used by encroaching settlers to appropriate Indian lands."**

> **"I am tired of fighting. Our chiefs are killed... It is cold and we have no blankets. The little children are freezing to death... Hear me, my chiefs, I am tired, my heart is sick and sad. From where the sun now stands I will fight no more forever."**
>
> **Nez Perce Chief Joseph - 1877**

Indian who did not represent the tribe or plying the negotiators with whiskey.

Hundreds of treaties were negotiated between Indians and European settlers from early colonial days to the establishment of the United States. In 1778, the United States government entered into its first official treaty with the Delawares. At least 370 documented treaties were negotiated during the next 100 years.

In 1871, Congress declared that no Indian nation would be recognized for the purpose of making treaties. By then, Indians realized that treaty negotiations had become a charade of empty promises based on fraud and deceit for the convenience of the government and the benefit of the land-hungry settlers.

An inherent stipulation in these treaty negotiations was the trust responsibility of the United State government to provide for the health, education and welfare of the Indian people. The general consensus in the Indian community is that government has not lived up to it's trust responsibilities. These issues have not been resolved to an equitable conclusion. Some Indian tribes are seeking reparations through the legal system.

VANQUISHED INDIANS

By 1890, the physically battered Indians were decimated. Those remaining were confined to desolate reservations with its daily regimen of hardships, humiliation and exploitation. The once fearsome warrior had been reduced to a despised beggar, thief and a nuisance. The reservation system served to keep Indians out of sight and under control. They essentially became wards of the government and their needs were given a very low priority.

The vanquished Indians became a favorite subject of the media. Their plight was compounded by the timely invention of motion pictures. The nation's concept of Indians was the indelible celluloid images created by Hollywood westerns for entertainment. Marauding savage hordes became villainous anti-heroes as they attacked hopelessly outnumbered courageous settlers. Indians became a maligned blur of fact and fiction. The movie blitz was so effective that most fictitious perceptions still exist today.

Recent movies such as "Dances With Wolves," "Black Robe," "Thunderheart" and "Incident at Oglala," are efforts to present a more realistic image of Indians. There are several ambitious documentary type TV and movie projects in production that, hopefully, will present a more accurate version of Indian history.

There is a movement by talented Indian people in the entertainment industry to organize and produce their own version of Indian history and stories. The movement is based on the premise that only Indians can tell Indian reality. Literature and productions about Indians can never take the place of literature and productions by Indians.

"Give me your tired, your poor, your huddled masses yearning to breathe free, the wretched refuse of your teeming shore. Send these, the homeless, tempest-tossed to me. I lift my lamp beside the golden door."

Statue of Liberty Inscription - 1903

➤ CHAPTER 2 • Indianology

> "We therefore ask you while you are teaching school children, teach them truth about the First Americans... Why not teach school children more of the wholesome proverbs and legends of our people? That we killed game only for food, not for fun... Tell your children of the friendly acts of Indians to the white people who first settled here. Tell them of our leaders and heroes and their deeds... Put in your history books the Indian's part in the World War. Tell how the Indian fought for a country of which he was not a citizen, for a flag to which had no claim, and for a people who treated him unjustly. We ask this, Chief, to keep sacred the memory or our people."
>
> **Grand Council Fire of American Indians to the Mayor of Chicago - 1927**

DEMOGRAPHIC GUIDELINES

The **Digest** will focus its attention on the last 500 years chronologically and the continental United States geographically. Alaska and Hawaii have unique circumstances that require specific knowledge and will be addressed at a future date.

The demographics of Indian population, tribes and reservations are complex and in perpetual transition. At the risk of oversimplification, the **Digest** will profile sufficient demographics to present a generalized perspective within a national frame of reference.

Demographics can never be an exact science because theoretically they change daily. People are born and die each day and people relocate every day. However, demographics do give us a sense of perspective. For our purposes, most of the time we have rounded the

"Demographics with regard to Indian population, tribes and reservations are extremely complex and in perpetual transition."

exact numbers to the next highest number so that they will be easier to remember conceptually. The exact numbers are available, but they are already 5 years old.

The full impact of computer technology on scientific discovery is beyond our comprehension at the moment. We have gained access to more information in the last 10 years, than in all of man's previously recorded history. Computer experts indicate that our information and knowledge will double every 3 to 4 years.

The computer age phenomenon affects our past and future information by greater scientific discovery to support or refute old theories and beliefs. It also provides us with the means for tremendous communication and networking opportunities.

Indian demographics are in the process of becoming part of the information age. Government agencies and private enterprise are hard at work developing CD-ROM programs that will generate this information through computer network downloading.

TribAl NATioNS

Each tribal history is a unique chapter in the book of Indianology.

Social scientists offer the premise that there may be other migration theories. For the purpose of our discussion, we will assume the prevalent theory that the Indian tribal pyramid began as hunters crossed the Bering Straits in Alaska and began their migration over two continents.

Indian tribes formed as part of a natural process which evolved over thousands of years. Indian lifestyles and the limitations of the environment determined the number of people that could live in a given area. Social and political differences were important factors in the development of splinter clans, bands and tribes.

"Indian tribes formed as part of a natural process which evolved over thousands of years."

The United States government's legal definition for Indian tribes: *"any Indian tribe, band, nation, rancheria, pueblo, colony or community which is recognized by the United States government as eligible for the special programs and services provided by the Secretary of the Interior to Indians because of their status as Indians."*

- 319 tribes are federally recognized in the continental United States.

- The spectrum ranges from several California tribal bands that have 2-3 members to the Cherokees of Oklahoma at 308,000.

- Approximately 200 tribes are extinct.

- Approximately 120 tribes are in various stages of petition for federal recognition. These tribes range in size from small bands to the Lumbees of North Carolina with over 40,000 members.

- Approximately 30 tribes are state recognized.

Generally speaking, today's tribal names are the result of mangled pronunciations or hybrid designations by early trappers and settlers. Several tribes have recently changed their official names to reflect tribal languages. The Papago to Tohono O'Odham, et al.

Jack D. Forbes, a professor at the University of California in Davis, California, published the "Atlas of Native History." A feature of the study lists the tribal names in their respective Indian language referenced to the English version of the same name.

Tribal Sovereignty

Each Indian tribe considers itself a sovereign nation. Most tribes have recently decided that the politically correct reference will be "nations" rather than tribes. The issue of sovereignty has been a subject of long-running debate between the United States government and the tribes. The United States government negotiated treaties with the tribes as sovereign nations and promised certain inalienable rights in exchange for land cessions.

By definition: Sovereignty is supreme and complete political independence and self-government. A sovereign nation must have the ability to defend its borders, exercise authority over it's citizens and conduct its business free from outside interference.

Tribal sovereignty is a paradox because the United States government, while recognizing the tribes as sovereign nations, has perpetuated a relationship of tribal dependence on the government.

- Does Chicken Ranch Rancheria in California at 3 acres and 10 Indians have the same sovereignty as the Navajo with 17 million acres and 220,000 people?

- Do tribal governments expect freedom from government paternalism and yet remain recipients of government Indian entitlement programs?

The Interior Department has recently caused concern in the Indian community by it's definition of "historic" tribes as those that have existed since time immemorial, whose powers derive from their unextinguished, inherent sovereignty. "Non-historic" tribes are those created under the 1934 Indian Reorganization Act that have only powers incidental to owning property and conducting business.

Population

There have been numerous studies regarding the Indian population when Columbus reached the New World. Most studies included North and South America with estimates that ranged from 5 to 30 million.

Eventually, technology will provide a more accurate estimate. Until then, a reasonable assumption is that there were approximately 1 million native inhabitants within the continental United States existing as some 500 tribes. The tribes varied in size from a few dozen to several thousand, speaking more than 300 languages.

Official Recognition

The government definition of a "legal" Indian is: *"Any person who has the certifiable Indian blood quantum to meet the enrollment requirements of a federally recognized tribe."* This seemingly innocuous definition has been the cause of enormous dilemma in the Indian community.

Indians are the only race of people who must legally prove that they are Indian. Other races are accepted at face value. Each tribe has the right to determine the minimum blood quantum requirements for enrollment. The result is that blood quantum requirements vary from tribe to tribe.

- At one end of the spectrum: the Cherokee Nation of Oklahoma is known for the most liberal enrollment. They accept anyone, who can trace their ancestry to tribal membership rolls completed in 1906, regardless of blood quantum. Some enrolled Cherokees have a minute trace of Indian blood. This policy has increased the Cherokee enrollment to over 308,000. Other Cherokee Tribes have more stringent enrollment requirements.

- At the other end of the spectrum: the Utes of Utah require 5/8 minimum blood quantum for membership.

- Most tribes require 1/4 minimum blood quantum for enrollment.

The Official Count

The Digest utilized the 1990 Census demographics

because they are compiled by experts with extensive resources and have official recognition.

In September 1993, The Racial Statistics Branch of the Bureau of the Census published a 17 page booklet titled: "We The First Americans." The booklet is a comprehensive profile of the American Indian population.

The Census Bureau is a tremendous resource. A bureau catalog "Hidden Treasures" lists a vast array of data resources in many forms and where to find it. The bureau periodically issues updated information and additional reports, and also has an education program that is a great resource for teaching materials.

- There are approximately 1.9 million self-identified Indians in the United States. (Self-identified means there was a box on the 1990 Census form that said Indian - if you marked the box, you were counted as Indian.)

- Of that 1.9 million - 1.2 million Indians are tribally enrolled. (The numbers indicate that 700,000 people consider themselves Indian but are not enrolled.)

- There are an estimated 10 to 15 million people who have a discernible degree of Indian blood, but have lost their tribal connection.

Blood Quantum Issues

Plains Indians had distinct physical features that were different from Indians in the Southwest and Northwest tribes looked different than Eastern tribes. Today, there is usually a core population of each tribe that still has some of those physically distinct features, but as mobility increased, the physical differences have become blurred.

Indians have mixed inter-tribally for thousands of

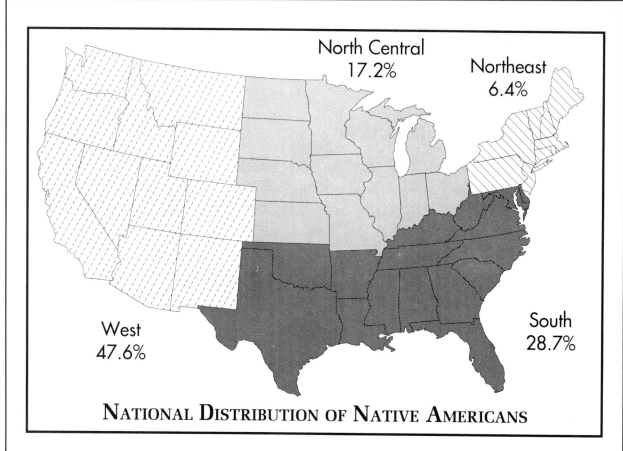

North Central
17.2%

Northeast
6.4%

West
47.6%

South
28.7%

NATIONAL DISTRIBUTION OF NATIVE AMERICANS

INDIAN POPULATION DEMOGRAPHICS

URBAN INDIAN POP. BY CITY

	City	Population
1.	Los Angeles	87,487
2.	Tulsa	48,196
3.	New York	46,191
4.	Oklahoma City	45,720
5.	San Francisco	40,847
6.	Phoenix	38,017
7.	Seattle-Tacoma	32,017
8.	Minneapolis	23,956
9.	Tucson	20,330
10.	San Diego	20,066

RESERVATION BY POPULATION

	Reservation	Population
1.	Navajo	148,451
2.	Pine Ridge	12,113
3.	Fort Apache	10,394
4.	Gila River	9,540
5.	Rosebud	9,696
6.	Tohono O'Odham	8,730
7.	Blackfeet	8,549
8.	Zuni	7,412
9.	Hopi	7,360
10.	San Carlos	7,294

1990 CENSUS - AMERICAN INDIAN POPULATION BY STATE

Rank	State	Indian Pop.	% of State	Rank	State	Indian Pop.	% of State
1	Oklahoma	252,420	8.0	27	New Jersey	14,970	0.2
2	California	242,164	0.8	28	Pennsylvania	14,733	0.1
3	Arizona	203,527	5.6	29	Idaho	13,780	1.4
4	New Mexico	134,355	8.9	30	Georgia	13,348	0.2
5	Washington	81,483	1.7	31	Maryland	12,972	0.3
6	North Carolina	80,155	1.2	32	Arkansas	12,773	0.5
7	Texas	65,877	0.4	33	Indiana	12,720	0.2
8	New York	62,651	0.3	34	Nebraska	12,410	0.8
9	Michigan	55,638	0.6	35	Massachusetts	12,241	0.2
10	South Dakota	50,575	7.3	36	Tennessee	10,039	0.2
11	Minnesota	49,909	1.1	37	Wyoming	9,479	2.1
12	Montana	47,679	6.0	38	Mississippi	8,525	0.3
13	Wisconsin	39,387	0.8	39	South Carolina	8,246	0.2
14	Oregon	38,496	1.4	40	Iowa	7,349	0.3
15	Florida	36,335	0.3	41	Connecticut	6,654	0.2
16	Colorado	27,776	0.8	42	Maine	5,998	0.5
17	North Dakota	25,917	4.1	43	Kentucky	5,769	0.2
18	Utah	24,283	1.4	44	Hawaii	5,099	0.5
19	Kansas	21,965	0.9	45	Rhode Island	4,071	0.4
20	Illinois	21,836	0.2	46	West Virginia	2,458	0.1
21	Ohio	20,358	0.2	47	New Hampshire	2,134	0.2
22	Missouri	19,835	0.4	48	Delaware	2,019	0.3
23	Nevada	19,637	1.6	49	Vermont	1,696	0.3
24	Louisiana	18,541	0.4	50	Washington DC	1,466	0.2
25	Alabama	16,506	0.4				
26	Virginia	15,282	0.2		TOTAL	1,873,536	100.0

years and inter-racially for the last 500 years. The result is many generations of mixed-blood Indians.

The question of who is and who isn't Indian has become a burning issue in Indian Country. Contrary to the stereotypical image, Indians come in all sizes, shapes and colors. At any major Indian pow wow, conference or trade show, the spectrum of skin color of the audience and participants will range from white to black.

A conservative estimate would be that 98% of the Indian population is tribally hyphenated (Ottawa-Chippewa) and 75% are also racially hyphenated (Ottawa-Chippewa-Irish-English).

> "Indians have mixed inter-tribally for thousands of years and inter-racially for the last 500 years. The result is many generations of mixed-blood Indians."

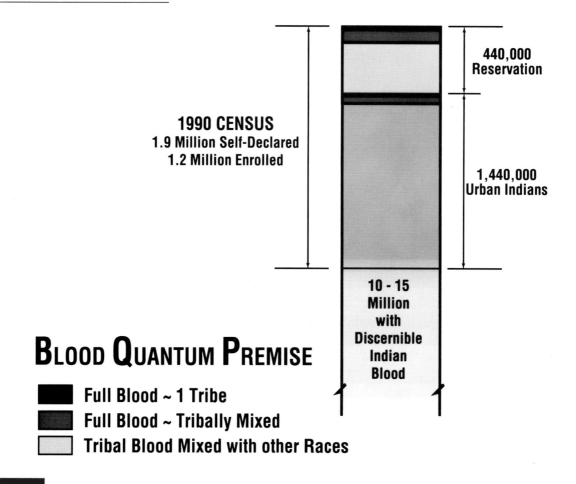

440,000
Reservation

1990 CENSUS
1.9 Million Self-Declared
1.2 Million Enrolled

1,440,000
Urban Indians

10 - 15
Million
with
Discernible
Indian
Blood

BLOOD QUANTUM PREMISE

■ Full Blood ~ 1 Tribe
■ Full Blood ~ Tribally Mixed
□ Tribal Blood Mixed with other Races

"Full Blood"

As Indians began the occupation of this part of the world, their origin was relatively singular and the prevalent theory is that they were one race of people.

The term "full-blood" is the designation for Indians who consider themselves to be 100% of one tribe. Is this possible or does "full-blood" at best mean composite tribal Indian blood? The designation seems to be more of a reference to spirituality and a traditional lifestyle than definitive blood quantum.

Tribally Mixed Bloods

Inter-tribal and clan mixing was a natural process to preclude genetic inbreeding. It was accepted custom to seek a mate from a neighboring tribe or clan. The creation of the reservation system and forced relocation of tribes accelerated the inter-tribal melting pot.

The most notorious example was the relocation of some 60 tribes from all parts of the country to Oklahoma territory during the 1800s.

Racially Mixed-Bloods

Settler, pioneer and frontier life in early America was a perilous regimen of hardships. Consequently, there was an acute shortage of European women. Because of the imbalance, sexual interaction between European men and Indian women was an inevitable and common practice.

Trappers, settlers and frontiersmen consorted with Indian women and often took Indian wives. The social attitude toward this practice was reflected by the term "squaw" and "squawman" with reference to Indian women and their European male counterparts. Within the context of the times, the designation "squaw" and "squawman" may have had various connotations, but the meaning was clear.

The attrition of time allowed the term "squaw" to

be commonly used as a generic reference to Indian women. The issue has become a point of contention in the Indian community and is no longer socially acceptable .

On the basis of this premise, there is the strong probability that there is Indian blood in the veins of a much larger segment of the population than was recorded or acknowledged. Since World War II, there is more of an inclination to acknowledge an Indian skeleton in the family closet.

The premise of racial blood mixing can be compared to the black slavery experience and the proliferation of mixed blood children as an aftermath of military occupation in foreign lands. Consensual and non-consensual sexual activity has always been a military prerogative during territorial conquest and occupation. Basic human nature will prevail. "The brotherhood of man", may be a much more appropriate expression than we realize.

Long-Term Ramifications

Two of the major issues facing Indian America with regard to the population and continuity of future generations that beg for resolution:

- The dilution of blood-quantum.

- Survival of urban Indians.

Blood quantum criteria is the cause of considerable division and inequities in the Indian community. An example: some Cherokees have a minute trace (such as 1/2048) of Indian blood and are enrolled, while other tribally mixed-bloods have considerable composite blood and are not enrolled because they do not meet any of their respective tribal blood quantum requirements.

Although, some tribes have modified their enrollment criteria to accept other composite Indian blood to

> **"Within the context of the times, the terms "squaw" and "squawman" had various connotations, but the meaning was clear."**

> **"Since World War II, there has been more of a propensity to acknowledge an Indian skeleton in the family closet."**

meet their respective enrollment quantum requirements, tribes do not allow membership in more than one tribe.

There are Indians whose families have been a part of Indian communities, sometimes for generations, who do not have official records required for certification.

Indian tribes did not have written languages, so during periods of relocation and assimilation, genealogy often became a matter of oral interpretation. Most Indian languages were difficult for Europeans to understand and pronounce, so a combination of oral and sign language became the basis for communication. As a result, Indians were often given arbitrary names and numbers for the records.

Reservation Indians

Indian population is further complicated by the evolution of two social categories: Reservation Indians and Urban Indians. For the most part, this division of Indians is a circumstance of birth.

Indians born on the reservation will generally stay on the reservation or return if they should leave. For Indians born off reservation, the chances of returning are remote, especially if the family migration happened generations ago and if there has been a geographic relocation.

This situation creates an internal dilemma: Reservation Indians receive the direct benefits of federal programs such as housing, utility subsistence, health care, education and economic development aid, while their enrolled urban counterparts are essentially excluded from most of these programs. Enrolled Urban Indians are included in the head count as a basis for procurement from these programs.

Urban Indians

From the turn of the century until World War II, Indians were subjected to the coercion of boarding schools, assimilation and relocation programs. The idea of this period of cultural genocide was to "kill the Indian and save the man."

During World War II, 25,000 Indians left the reservations to serve in the armed forces. After the war, migrations accelerated by choice to seek employment, education and opportunity.

Composition of today's urban Indian community:

- Enrolled members who live and work off reservation, but are still closely connected by family and sometimes have a reservation residence.

- Geographically relocated enrolled "at large" members by lineal descent or affiliated by marriage.

- People who have an Indian ancestor and are not enrolled, but are active in the Indian community and consider themselves Indians traditionally and spiritually.

- People who have an Indian ancestor - generations removed who have lost their tribal connection and are not active in the Indian community.

Most reservation Indians and urban Indians have close family ties and interact culturally. Many urban Indians live near their respective reservations.

According to the 1990 Census there are:

- 437,000 (437,431) reservation Indians. (22% of the total population.)

- 1,436,000 (1,436,105) urban Indians. (78% of the total population.)

It's understood that there is no solution that will satisfy or include everyone. The cold hard fact of life is that some people are going to be excluded who should be included and some people will be included who should be excluded. Do the issues have black and white answers or does the solution lie in the gray area of compromise?

RESERVATIONS

An Indian reservation is an area of land held in trust by the federal government reserved for Indian use. The Secretary of the Interior is the trustee for the United States. The Bureau of Indian Affairs (BIA) is responsible to the trustee for administration and management of Indian trust lands.

- Over 300 reservations are federally recognized totaling some 55 million acres.

- 44 million acres are tribal trust lands.

- 11 million acres are individually owned.

- There are approximately 30 state recognized reservations.

Indian trust lands range in size from some California rancherias of less than 1 acre to the Navajo Nation at more than 17 million acres.

A few reservations are nearly 100% tribal trust lands and others are almost entirely owned by individuals.

Some Indian tribes have an impressive array of resources on their trust lands. It seems poetic justice that some of the desolate reservations have become valuable land due to minerals resources, pristine resources and urban locations.

Reservation Resources:

- 44.0 million acres in range and grazing.
- 5.3 million acres of commercial forest.

"It seems poetic justice that some of the desolate reservations have become valuable land due to minerals resources, pristine resources and urban locations."

- 2.5 million acres of crop area.

- 4% of US oil & gas reserves.

- 40% of US uranium deposits.

- 30% of western coal reserves.

- $2 billion in trust royalty payments.

Historically, Indians have been allowed to occupy lands until an economic and or political requisition is mandated. The cultivated lands of the five "civilized tribes" in the Southeastern states, discovery of gold in the Black Hills of South Dakota, and the discovery of oil in Oklahoma are explicit examples. The 220 year history of Indians versus the United States government speaks for itself. **Congress giveth and Congress can taketh away.**

The 1830 Removal Act precipitated the infamous "Trail of Tears" that refers to the 1838 forced march of some 15,000 Cherokee Indians from their coveted farmlands in the Southeastern United States to Oklahoma Indian territory. More than 4,000 Indians died during the march from disease, exposure and starvation.

In a broader context, the "Trail of Tears" was typical of the forced removal of some 60,000 members of the five "Civilized Tribes" that lasted for nearly 10 years.

- Cherokee   • Creek   • Chickasaw
- Choctaw   • Seminole

The forced removal was in violation of a Supreme Court decision by Chief Justice John Marshall in favor of the Indians to which President Andrew Jackson responded, "John Marshall has made his decision, now let him enforce it."

Oklahoma territory became the final destination for some 60 tribes during the 1800s. Some of the major tribes are shown on the graphic on the next page.

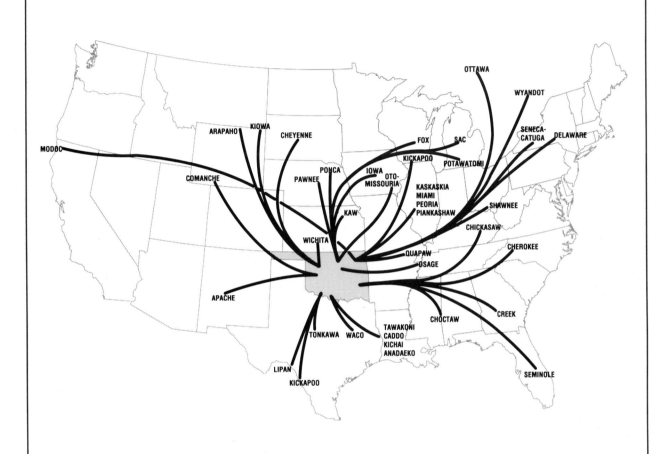

The large concentration of tribes relocated to Oklahoma came from a wide range of geographic areas. Consequently, Oklahoma Indian history presents a much larger view of Indian America than is indicated by the geographic area.

The Oklahoma Indian Affairs Commission has compiled a comprehensive report, "Histories & Statistical Information on Oklahoma's Resident Tribes & Nations." The report is referenced on page 68.

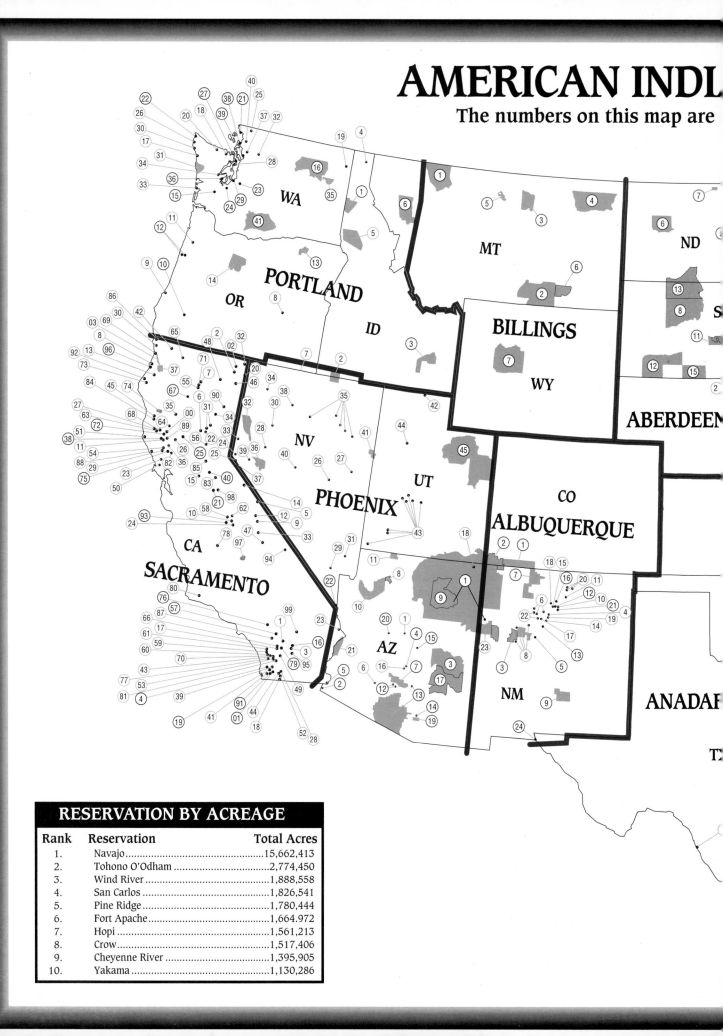

AMERICAN INDI

The numbers on this map are

RESERVATION BY ACREAGE

Rank	Reservation	Total Acres
1.	Navajo	15,662,413
2.	Tohono O'Odham	2,774,450
3.	Wind River	1,888,558
4.	San Carlos	1,826,541
5.	Pine Ridge	1,780,444
6.	Fort Apache	1,664.972
7.	Hopi	1,561,213
8.	Crow	1,517,406
9.	Cheyenne River	1,395,905
10.	Yakama	1,130,286

RESERVATIONS

...ced to the reservation roster.

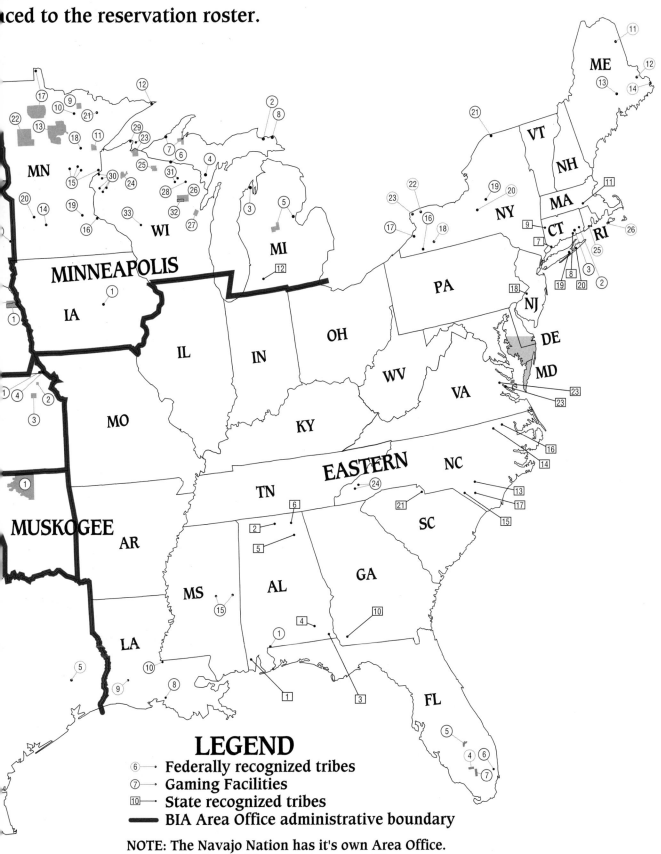

LEGEND
- ⑥ — Federally recognized tribes
- ⑦ — Gaming Facilities
- ⑩ — State recognized tribes
- ▬ BIA Area Office administrative boundary

NOTE: The Navajo Nation has it's own Area Office.
BIA Area Offices chart on page 71.

➤ RESERVATION ROSTER

Gross Acreage and Trust Land numbers are from the "Annual Report of Indian Lands" dated September 30, 1985. It is the most recent data available from the BIA.
Total Population and Indian Population numbers are from the 1990 Census.
... Indicates data was not available.
● Indicates Gaming Facilities.

	#	Nations	State	Gross Acreage	Trust Land	Total Pop.	Indian Pop.	Enrolled Pop.
		PORTLAND AREA OFFICE						
●	1	Coeur d'Alene	ID	67,981	21,268	5,802	749	
	2	Duck Valley	ID	289,819	289,819	1,101	1,022	
●	3	Fort Hall	ID	522,510	260,837	5,114	3,035	
	4	Kootenai	ID	1,825	183		85	130
	5	Nez Perce	ID	85,661	36,409	16,160	1,863	
	6	Flathead	MT	627,070	581,907	21,259	5,130	
	7	Fort McDermitt	NV-OR	16,497	0	396	387	
	8	Burns Paiute	OR	771	0	163	123	258
	9	Coos, Lower Umpqua & Siuslaw	OR	7	7	4	0	523
●	10	Cow Creek	OR	28	28	58	11	
	11	Grand Ronde	OR	9,811	9,811	57	1	
●	12	Siletz	OR	3,673	3,673	5	0	2,267
●	13	Umatilla	OR	44,000	18,000	2,502	984	1,489
	14	Warm Springs	OR	643,507	592,143	3,076	2,820	
●	15	Chehalis	WA	2,076	76	491	308	
●	16	Colville	WA	1,063,043	1,023,640	6,957	3,788	
	17	Hoh	WA	443	443	96	74	
	18	Jamestown Klallam	WA	11	8	22	4	
	19	Kalispel	WA	4,557	1,970	100	91	
	20	Lower Elwah	WA	427	427	137	130	
●	21	Lummi	WA	7,678	635	3,147	1,594	
●	22	Makah	WA	27,244	24,967	1,214	940	
●	23	Muckleshoot	WA	1,275	106	3,841	864	
●	24	Nisqually	WA	930	195	578	365	
	25	Nooksack	WA	10	10	0	0	1,250
	26	Ozette	WA	719	719	12	0	
●	27	Port Gamble	WA	1,303	1,303	552	377	
	28	Port Madison	WA	7,811	252	4,834	276	728
●	29	Puyallup	WA	18,000	500	32,406	937	1,700
	30	Quileute	WA	814	804	381	303	
	31	Quinault	WA	129,221	7,466	1,216	943	
	32	Sauk-Suiettle	WA	23	23	124	69	
	33	Shoalwater	WA	335	335	131	66	
	34	Skokomish	WA	2,987	162	614	431	
●	35	Spokane	WA	133,302	105,383	1,502	1,229	

#	Nations	State	Gross Acreage	Trust Land	Total Pop.	Indian Pop.	Enrolled Pop.
● 36	Squaxin Island	WA	971	145	157	127	
37	Stillaquamish	WA	0	0	113	96	
● 38	Swinomish	WA	6,400	1,600	2,282	425	525
● 39	Tulalip	WA	10,667	7,511	7,103	1,204	
40	Upper Skagit	WA	74	74	180	162	
41	Yakama	WA	1,130,286	904,411	27,668	6,307	

SACRAMENTO AREA OFFICE

#	Nations	State	Gross Acreage	Trust Land	Total Pop.	Indian Pop.	Enrolled Pop.
1	Aqua Caliente	CA	23,173	2,139	20,206	117	
2	Alturas Rancheria	CA	39	0		7	13
3	Augustine	CA	502	342	0	0	
● 4	Barona Rancheria	CA	5,922	5,922	537	373	325
5	Benton Paiute	CA	160	160	63	52	
6	Berry Creek Rancheria	CA	33	33	2	2	
7	Big Bend Rancheria	CA	40	40	3	3	
8	Big Lagoon Rancheria	CA	20	9	22	19	
9	Big Pine	CA	279	279	452	331	
10	Big Sandy Rancheria	CA	76	0	51	38	
11	Big Valley	CA	38	38	108	90	
12	Bishop Reservation	CA	875	875	1,408	1,300	
13	Blue Lake Rancheria	CA	4	0	58	30	
14	Bridgeport Indian Colony	CA	40	40	49	37	
15	Buena Vista	CA	0	0	1	1	
● 16	Cabazon	CA	1,382	954	819	20	
17	Cahuilla	CA	18,884	18,272	104	82	
18	Campo Reservation	CA	15,480	15,010	281	143	
● 19	Capitain Grande	CA	15,753	15,753	0	0	
20	Cedarville Rancheria	CA	20	17	8	6	
● 21	Chicken Ranch Rancheria	CA	30,654	3	73	10	
22	Chico Rancheria	CA	0	0	0	0	
23	Cloverdale Rancheria	CA	19	0	1	1	
24	Cold Springs Rancheria	CA	155	155	192	159	
● 25	Colusa Rancheria	CA	273	0	22	19	
26	Cortina Rancheria	CA	640	640	30	22	
27	Coyote Valley Rancheria	CA	58	58	135	122	
28	Cuyapaipe	CA	4,103	4,100	0	0	
29	Dry Creek Rancheria	CA	75	75	75	38	
30	Elk Valley Rancheria	CA	100	48	77	82	260
31	Enterprise Rancheria	CA	40	40	5	5	
32	Ft Bidwell	CA	3,335	3,335	118	107	
33	Ft Independence	CA	234	234	69	38	
34	Greenville Rancheria	CA	0	0	24	7	
35	Grindstone Rancheria	CA	80	80	103	102	
36	Guidiville Rancheria	CA	0	0	0	0	
37	Hoopa Valley	CA	93,000	85,000	2,143	1,733	2.022
● 38	Hopland Rancheria	CA	48	22	189	142	
39	Inaja-Cosmit	CA	852	852	0	0	
● 40	Jackson Rancheria	CA	331	331	21	13	
41	Jamul Indian Village	CA	6	6	0	0	
42	Karuk Tribe	CA	243	18	1,096	0	2,092
43	La Jolla	CA	8,541	7,588	152	121	
44	La Posta	CA	3,556	3,672	10	3	

#	Nations	State	Gross Acreage	Trust Land	Total Pop.	Indian Pop.	Enrolled Pop.
45	Laytonville Rancheria	CA	200	200	142	129	
46	Likely Rancheria	CA	1	1	0	0	
47	Lone Pine	CA	237	237	244	168	
48	Lookout Rancheria	CA	40	40	17	12	
49	Los Coyotes Rancheria	CA	25,049	25,049	58	42	
50	Lytton Rancheria	CA	0	0	0	0	
51	Manchester Point Rancheria	CA	363	363	200	178	
52	Manzanita	CA	3,579	3,579	84	47	
53	Mesa Grande	CA	1,000	1,000	96	95	335
54	Middletown Rancheria	CA	109	109	79	18	
55	Montgomery Creek Rancheria	CA	72	72	11	9	
56	Mooretown	CA	0	0	225	0	
● 57	Morongo	CA	32,362	30,968	1,072	527	
58	North Fork Rancheria	CA	80	0	4	0	
59	Pala	CA	11,893	10,319	1,071	563	
60	Pauma & Yuima	CA	5,877	5,877	148	137	
61	Pechanga	CA	4,394	2,626	398	289	
62	Picayune Rancheria	CA	29	0	32	15	
63	Pinoleville Rancheria	CA	3	3	130	77	
64	Potter Valley Rancheria	CA	3	3	1	1	
65	Quartz Valley Rancheria	CA	24	0	124	19	
66	Ramona	CA	560	560	0	0	
● 67	Redding Rancheria	CA	31	0	101	79	
68	Redwood Valley Rancheria	CA	170	170	142	14	
69	Resighini Rancheria	CA	228	228	28	26	
70	Rincon	CA	4,276	3,612	1,352	379	
71	Roaring Creek Rancheria	CA	80	80	18	18	
● 72	Robinson Rancheria	CA	103	68	139	113	
73	Rohnerville Rancheria	CA	0	0	8	8	
74	Round Valley	CA	30,538	13,601	1,183	577	
● 75	Rumsey Rancheria	CA	185	185	35	35	35
● 76	San Manuel	CA	658	658	80	56	
77	San Pasqual	CA	1,380	1,380	512	212	
78	Santa Rosa Rancheria	CA	170	179	323	284	
● 79	Santa Rosa	CA	11,093	11,093	50	37	
80	Santa Ynez	CA	127	127	279	213	
81	Santa Ysabel	CA	15,527	15,527	169	150	
82	Scotts Valley Rancheria	CA	57	0	140	92	
83	Sheep Ranch Rancheria	CA	1	1	0	0	
84	Sherwood Valley Rancheria	CA	350	292	15	9	
85	Shingle Springs Rancheria	CA	160	160	18	7	
86	Smith River Rancheria	CA	91	25	200		689
87	Soboba	CA	5,916	5,036	369	308	
88	Stewart's Point Rancheria	CA	40	40	91	86	
89	Sulphur Bank Rancheria	CA	50	50	93	90	
90	Susanville Rancheria	CA	150	150	454	154	
● 91	Sycuan	CA	640	371	4	0	
92	Table Bluff Rancheria	CA	0	0	48	43	
● 93	Table Mountain Rancheria	CA	61	37	51	48	
94	Timbi-Sha W. Shoshon	CA	40	40	55	55	270
95	Torres-Martinez	CA	24,024	18,223	4,462	143	

#	Nations	State	Gross Acreage	Trust Land	Total Pop.	Indian Pop.	Enrolled Pop.
● 96	Trinidad Rancheria	CA	47	44	78	59	
97	Tule River	CA	55,356	55,356	798	745	
98	Tuolumne Rancheria	CA	336	336	135	107	
99	Twenty-Nine Palms	CA	402	402	0	0	
100	Upper Lake Rancheria	CA	19	0	76	28	
● 101	Viejas	CA	1,609	1,609	411	227	
102	XL Ranch	CA	9,255	9,255	35	27	
103	Yurok Tribe	CA	3,669	3,669	1,357	463	

PHOENIX AREA OFFICE

#	Nations	State	Gross Acreage	Trust Land	Total Pop.	Indian Pop.	Enrolled Pop.
1	Camp Verde	AZ	653	653	618	569	
● 2	Cocopah	AZ	6,009	6,009	515	436	
3	Fort Apache	AZ	?	?	10,394	9,825	
● 4	Fort McDowell	AZ	24,680	24,680	640	560	816
● 5	Fort Yuma	AZ-CA	43,561	35,435	2,084	1,160	
6	Gila Bend	AZ	10,404	10,404	0	0	
● 7	Gila River	AZ	371,933	274,278	9,540	9,116	
8	Havasupai	AZ	188,077	188,077	423	400	
9	Hopi	AZ	1,561,213	1,560,993	7,360	7,061	
10	Hualapai	AZ	992,463	992,463	822	802	
11	Kaibab	AZ	120,413	120,413	165	102	
● 12	Maricopa(Ak-Chin)	AZ	21,840	21,840	446	405	
● 13	Tohono O'Odham(Papago)	AZ	2,800,000	2,490,065		11,038	17,678
● 14	Pascua Yaqui	AZ	895	895	2,412	2,284	
● 15	Payson Community	AZ	85	85	102	97	
16	Salt River	AZ	50,506	26,072	4,852	3,533	5,430
● 17	San Carlos	AZ	1,826,541	1,826,541	7,294	7,110	
18	San Juan Southern Paiute	AZ	0	0	204	204	
● 19	San Xavier	AZ	71,095	30,412	1,172	1,073	
● 20	Yavapai	AZ	1,398	1,398	176	134	
21	Colorado River	AZ-CA	225,995	220,116	7,865	2,345	
● 22	Fort Mojave	AZ-CA-NV	32,697	32,697	758	592	
23	Chemehuevi	CA	30,654	30,654	358	95	
24	Carson Colony	NV	160	160	248	235	
25	Dresslerville Colony	NV	40	40	152	144	
26	Duckwater	NV	3,815	3,815	135	115	
27	Ely Colony	NV	100	100	59	52	
28	Fallon Colony	NV	8,180	3,540	546	506	
29	Las Vegas Colony	NV	3,723	3,723	80	72	
30	Lovelock Colony	NV	20	20	94	80	
31	Moapa River	NV	71,955	71,955	375	190	
32	Pyramid Lake	NV	476,689	476,689	1,388	959	
33	Reno-Sparks Colony	NV	1,984	1,984	264	262	747
34	Summit Lake	NV	10,863	10,098	7	6	
35	Te-Moak	NV	13,050	13,050	949	831	
36	Walker River	NV	323,406	313,690	802	620	
37	Washoe	NV	3,672	3,672	157	65	
38	Winnemucca Colony	NV	340	340	67	61	
39	Yerington	NV	1,632	0	428	324	

#	Nations	State	Gross Acreage	Trust Land	Total Pop.	Indian Pop.	Enrolled Pop.
40	Yomba	NV	4,718	4,718	95	88	
41	Goshute	NV-UT	7,489	0	99	98	
42	Northwestern Shoshoni	UT	0	0	0	0	
43	Paiute	UT	425	425	645	323	
44	Skull Valley	UT	17,445	17,284	32	32	
45	Uintah & Ouray	UT	1,021,558	1,007,238	17,224	2,650	

NAVAJO AREA OFFICE

#	Nations	State	Gross Acreage	Trust Land	Total Pop.	Indian Pop.	Enrolled Pop.
1	Navajo	AZ-NM-UT	17,213,941	14,833,137	191,608	160,000	220,000
2	Alamo(Navajo)	NM	63,108	43,335	1,271	1,228	
3	Canoncito(Navajo)	NM	76,813	68,144	1,189	1,177	
4	Ramah Community(Navajo)	NM	146,953	99,353	194	191	

ALBUQUERQUE AREA OFFICE

	#	Nations	State	Gross Acreage	Trust Land	Total Pop.	Indian Pop.	Enrolled Pop.
●	1	Southern Ute	CO	310,002	307,561	7,804	1,044	
●	2	Ute Mountain	CO-NM-UT	477,850	477,850	1,320	1,264	
●	3	Acoma Pueblo	NM	263,611	263,291	2,590	2,551	
	4	Cochiti Pueblo	NM	50,669	50,669	1,342	666	
●	5	Isleta Pueblo	NM	211,034	211,026	2,915	2,699	
	6	Jemez Pueblo	NM	89,619	89,617	1,750	1,738	
●	7	Jicarilla Apache	NM	823,580	823,580	2,617	2,375	
	8	Laguna Pueblo	NM	461,099	458,933	3,731	3,634	
●	9	Mescalero Apache	NM	460,678	460,678	2,695	2,516	
	10	Nambe Pueblo	NM	19,076	19,076	1,402	329	
	11	Picuris Pueblo	NM	14,947	14,947	1,882	147	
●	12	Pojoaque Pueblo	NM	1,842	12	2,556	180	231
●	13	Sandia Pueblo	NM	22,871	22,871	3,971	358	
	14	San Felipe Pueblo	NM	48,930	48,859	2,434	1,859	
	15	San Ildefonso Pueblo	NM	26,198	26,196	1,499	347	
●	16	San Juan Pueblo	NM	12,237	12,235	5,209	1,276	
	17	Santa Ana Pueblo	NM	61,414	61,414	593	481	
	18	Santa Clara Pueblo	NM	45,748	45,744	10,193	1,246	
	19	Santo Domingo Pueblo	NM	69,260	69,260	2,992	2,947	
	20	Taos Pueblo	NM	95,341	95,334	4,745	1,212	
●	21	Tesuque Pueblo	NM	16,813	16,811	697	232	
	22	Zia Pueblo	NM	117,680	117,680	637	637	
	23	Zuni Pueblo	NM-AZ	409,182	406,969	7,412	7,073	
●	24	Ysleta Del Sur Puebl	TX	67	67	3,300	3,305	1,463

ANADARKO AREA OFFICE

	#	Nations	State	Gross Acreage	Trust Land	Total Pop.	Indian Pop.	Enrolled Pop.
●	1	Iowa	KS	1,072	866	172	83	
●	2	Kickapoo	KS	6,660	3,505	478	370	
●	3	Pottawatomi	KS	21,479	2,939	279	502	
●	4	Sac & Fox	KS-NE	354	309	210	49	
	5	Alabama-Coushatta	TX	4,600	4,600	478	477	

#	Nations	State	Gross Acreage	Trust Land	Total Pop.	Indian Pop.	Enrolled Pop.
6	Kickapoo	TX	0	0	0	0	

MUSKOGEE AREA OFFICE

#	Nations	State	Gross Acreage	Trust Land	Total Pop.	Indian Pop.	Enrolled Pop.
● 1	Osage	OK	168,794	675	41,645	6,161	

BILLINGS AREA OFFICE

#	Nations	State	Gross Acreage	Trust Land	Total Pop.	Indian Pop.	Enrolled Pop.
1	Blackfeet	MT	937,838	302,072	8,549	7,025	14,146
● 2	Crow	MT	1,517,406	408,444	6,370	4,724	8,954
● 3	Fort Belknap	MT	588,756	188,017	2,508	2,338	5,075
● 4	Fort Peck	MT	904,683	391,769	10,595	5,782	10,047
● 5	Rocky Boy's	MT	108,334	108,334	1,954	1,882	4,522
● 6	Northern Cheyenne	MT	436,948	318,072	3,923	3,542	6,388
7	Wind River	WY	1,888,558	1,793,420	21,851	5,676	8,001

ABERDEEN AREA OFFICE

#	Nations	State	Gross Acreage	Trust Land	Total Pop.	Indian Pop.	Enrolled Pop.
● 1	Omaha Reservation	NE-IA	26,792	9,596	5,227	1,908	
2	Ponca	NE	0	0	0	0	
3	Santee Sioux	NE	9,358	6,943	758	425	
● 4	Winnebago	NE-IA	27,538	4,241	2,341	1,156	
● 5	Devils Lake Sioux	ND	53,239	16,229	3,588	2,676	
6	Fort Berthold	ND	419,362	69,509	5,395	2,999	
● 7	Turtle Mountain	ND	46,080	8,807		9,819	25,005
● 8	Cheyenne River	SD	1,395,905	954,398	7,743	5,100	
9	Crow Creek	SD	125,483	65,018	1,756	1,531	
● 10	Flandreau Santee Sioux	SD	2,183	3,183	279	249	
● 11	Lower Brule	SD	130,239	104,244	1,123	994	
● 12	Pine Ridge	SD-NE	1,780,444	709,112	12,215	11,182	
● 13	Standing Rock	SD-ND	847,254	356,039	7,956	4,870	
● 14	Sisseton-Wahpeton	SD-ND	105,543	17,104	10,733	2,821	
15	Rosebud	SD	954,572	529,954	9,696	8,043	
● 16	Yankton	SD	36,559	16,706	6,269	1,994	

MINNEAPOLIS AREA OFFICE

#	Nations	State	Gross Acreage	Trust Land	Total Pop.	Indian Pop.	Enrolled Pop.
● 1	Sac & Fox	IA	3,540	9,479	577	564	2,243
● 2	Bay Mills	MI	2,209	2,209	461	403	915
● 3	Grand Traverse	MI	0	0	228	208	1,702
● 4	Hannahville Community	MI	412	3,411	3,411	181	408
● 5	Isabella	MI	138,240	676	22,944	795	2,099
● 6	Lac Vieux Desert	MI	104	104	124	119	215
● 7	L'Anse	MI	13,765	5,764	3,293	724	412
● 8	Sault Ste. Marie	MI	293	293	768	554	22,593
● 9	Nett Lake	MN	41,864	30,354	358	346	
● 10	Fond du Lac	MN	21,932	4,898	3,229	1,106	
● 11	Grand Portage	MN	44,844	37,679	306	207	

43

#	Nations	State	Gross Acreage	Trust Land	Total Pop.	Indian Pop.	Enrolled Pop.
12	Leech Lake	MN	677,099	16,123	8,669	3,725	7,085
13	Lower Sioux Community	MN	1,745	1,745	259	225	
14	Mille Lacs	MN	61,000	4,000	470	1,200	2,663
15	Prairie Island Community	MN	571	571	60	56	
16	Red Lake	MN	837,845	837,845	3,699	5,000	7,829
17	Shakopee	MN	293	293	203	153	
18	Upper Sioux Community	MN	745	745	49	43	
19	White Earth	MN	56,078	54,125	8,727	2,759	
20	Bad River	WI	56,558	23,451	1,070	868	
21	Lac Courte Oreilles	WI	48,139	22,062	2,408	1,771	
22	Lac du Flambeau	WI	44,726	30,344	2,434	1,432	
23	Menominee	WI	222,552	222,552	3,397	3,182	
24	Oneida	WI	2,751	2,366	18,033	2,447	
25	Potawatomi	WI	11,692	11,292	1,082	266	
26	Red Cliff	WI	7,495	5,458	857	727	
27	St. Croix	WI	1,940	1,940	505	462	
28	Sokaogon Chippewa Community	WI	1,694	1,694	357	311	1,552
29	Stockbridge	WI	15,603	15,447	581	447	
30	Wisconsin Winnebago	WI	4,245	632	700	570	

EASTERN AREA OFFICE

#	Nations	State	Gross Acreage	Trust Land	Total Pop.	Indian Pop.	Enrolled Pop.
1	Poarch Creek	AL					2,000
2	Mashantucket Pequot	CT	3,073	1,229	83	180	262
3	Mohegan Nation	CT	700	700	1,600	35	600
4	Big Cypress	FL	42,728	42,728	484	447	
5	Brighton	FL	35,805	35,805	524	402	
6	Hollywood	FL	481	481	1,394	481	
7	Miccosukee	FL	75,146	74,812	94	94	
8	Chitimacha	LA	283	283	286	212	
9	Coushatta	LA	154	154	36	33	
10	Tunica-Biloxi	LA	134	134	29	16	
11	Aroostook Band	ME	0	0	0	0	
12	Indian Township	ME	23,000	23,000	617	541	
13	Penobscot	ME	127,838	60,143	517	430	
14	Pleasant Point	ME	200	200	572	523	
15	Mississippi Choctaw	MS	17,926	17,715	4,073	3,932	6,000
16	Allegany	NY	30,984	0	7,315	1,062	
17	Cattaraugus	NY	22,013	0	2,178	2,051	
18	Oil Springs	NY	640	0	5	0	
19	Oneida	NY	32	0	37	37	
20	Onondaga	NY	7,300	0	771	2	
21	St. Regis Mohawk	NY	14,640	0	1,978	1,923	
22	Tonawanda	NY	495	0	501	453	

#	Nations	State	Gross Acreage	Trust Land	Total Pop.	Indian Pop.	Enrolled Pop.
23	Tuscarora	NY	5,778	0	772	310	
24	Eastern Cherokee	NC	56,573	56,461	6,527	5,388	
25	Narragansett	RI	0	0	31	17	
26	Wampanoag	RI					

STATE RECOGNIZED TRIBES

There are numerous Indian communities that do not have state or federal recognition. According to the List of Tribal Petitioners there are approximate 120 tribes that have pending applications for federal recognition.

State recognition is less rigorous and seems to be a milestone toward federal recognition. We have not been able to locate a national roster of state recognized tribes. As state recognized tribes come to our attention, they are added to this roster.

#	Nations	State	Gross Acreage	Trust Land	Total Pop.	Indian Pop.	Enrolled Pop.
1	MOWA Band of Choctaw	AL					7,000
2	Echota Cherokee	AL					20,000
3	Cherokee of Southeast Alabama	AL					500
4	MaChis Lower Creek Tribe	AL					850
5	Star Clan of Muscoge Creeks	AL					2,500
6	Cherokee of Northeast Alabama	AL					
7	Golden Hill Paugussett	CT	0	0	5	5	
8	Paucatuck Eastern Pequot	CT	0	0	18	15	
9	Schaghticoke	CT	0	0	10	7	
10	Tama	GA	0	0	22	16	
11	Hassanamisco	MA	0	0	1	1	
12	Pine Creek	MI	0	0	24	20	
13	Coharie	NC					
14	Haliwa-Saponi	NC					
15	Lumbee	NC					40,000
16	Meherrin	NC					
17	Waccamaw-Siouan	NC					
18	Rankokus	NJ	0	0	0	0	
19	Poospatuck	NY	0	0	136	95	
20	Shinnecock	NY			375	339	
21	Catawba	SC	0	0	174	124	1,250
22	Mattaponi	VA	0	0	70	65	
23	Pamunkey	VA	0	0	49	35	

➤ CHAPTER 3 • Indian Reality

American Indians Today

Almost everyone agrees that Indians have legitimate grievances that have not been equitably resolved, however, most Indian issues are obscured by current national and international crises.

To establish a realistic perspective, list the country's major domestic and foreign problems. Rank them in some order of priority, beginning with AIDS, third world starvation, homelessness, drugs, unemployment, education, health care, space programs, military defense, environmental pollution - the list is endless. Now rank Indian issues on that list.

Congress is the political and economic power base of the country and Congress is motivated by a combination of politics, economics, public opinion and lobbied interests. There are few Indian advocates in Congress. The issue is aptly stated by Senator DeConcini of Arizona who says from a congressional perspective: *"Nobody gives a damn about Indians."*

Although major Indian civilizations had flourished centuries before the white man's arrival, Indian cultures were not recognized by Europeans as established civilizations. Nor have they been given the appropriate recognition for their significant contributions to the development of this country.

Indian issues are emotionally charged and logic is often clouded by the heat of the moment. It is very difficult to be objective. Attitude and the law are often a matter of convenience and purpose as the United States government justifies its treatment of Indians.

The dilemma is compounded by social complacency and misinformation. Negative stereotyping is still

> **"The issue is aptly stated by Senator DeConcini of Arizona who says from a congressional perspective:** *"Nobody gives a damn about Indians."*

prevalent today and serves as an effective conduit for discrimination and prejudice that leads to exploitation. Neither attitudes nor morality can be legislated; they can only be formed through education.

Adaptability is fundamental to most Indian problems. Indians are polarized between tradition and culture on one hand and adaptation to the progress of the dominant culture on the other. The issue seems to be the appropriate degree of adaptability.

Obviously, a lessor degree of adaptability is required from an Indian living a traditional lifestyle on the reservation than from an Indian professional living in Phoenix. These are the extremes with a spectrum of reservation and urban lifestyles between.

Even traditional reservation Indians have adapted to some degree. Horses, guns and clothing were early adaptations. Modern home construction, electricity, running water, automobiles, television and telephone are evidence of more recent adaptation.

Being Indian is not only a matter of blood quantum, it is a mindset and a spirituality. Traditionally, Indian spirituality is an integral part of living in harmony with the rhythms of nature.

Historically, most Indian tribes were primarily a migratory people. The migrations were dictated by the laws of nature and, more recently, by the mandates of the dominant society. A cultural consequence of these migrations is an attachment of spiritual significance to geographic features.

Each urban Indian must determine what degree of adaptation is required to function as a productive member of society and yet preserve their Indian nature. Some Indians wear long hair, braids, jewelry and apparel as a declaration while others use some or none of the trappings.

Nothing is forever and the only thing for sure is

"Evolution is an absolute for the survival of a species or a civilization. Adaptability is the daily form of evolution."

change. Indians are a very small minority (1.2 million) that are a step behind mainstream society by all socio-economic standards. They are clinging to a past-life and may even be morally and ecologically correct. However, life moves on and we are witness to the winds of change because it is a natural order.

Indian Reality

The United States is outraged at oppression and abuse of indigenous people in other countries, while at home American Indians are a dispossessed and disenfranchised people in their own land. The hypocrisy should be an embarrassment to the country that is considered the world leader of democracy and guardian of human rights. It is incumbent upon the United States government to set an example for the world with regard to treatment of their respective native inhabitants.

Indians have made tremendous progress in recent years, but are still the poorest race in the country with regard to health, education and welfare. The majority of American Indians do not share in the American dream. The following conditions are a matter of record:

Health

- Fetal alcohol syndrome (FAS) is 33 times higher than non-Indians.

- 1 in 6 adolescents has attempted suicide - a rate four times that of other teenagers.

- Alcohol mortality is 10 times the rate for all other races combined.

- Tuberculosis is 7.4 times greater than non-Indians.

- Diabetes is 6.8 times greater than non-Indians.

"No democracy can long survive which does not accept as fundamental to its very existence the recognition of the rights of minorities."

Franklin D. Roosevelt
(1882-1945)

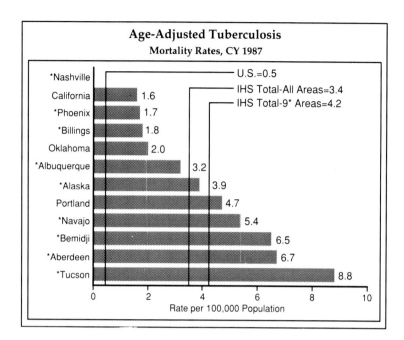

Age-Adjusted Tuberculosis
Mortality Rates, CY 1987

- U.S.=0.5
- IHS Total-All Areas=3.4
- IHS Total-9* Areas=4.2

Area	Rate
*Nashville	
California	1.6
*Phoenix	1.7
*Billings	1.8
Oklahoma	2.0
*Albuquerque	3.2
*Alaska	3.9
Portland	4.7
*Navajo	5.4
*Bemidji	6.5
*Aberdeen	6.7
*Tucson	8.8

Rate per 100,000 Population

In 1987, the age-adjusted tuberculosis mortality rate for the IHS service area population was 3.4. When the 3 IHS Areas with apparent problems in underreporting of Indian race on death certificates are excluded, the rate is 4.2. This is 740 percent higher than the U.S. All Races rate of 0.5. Some of the Area rates should be interpreted with caution because of the small number of deaths involved. The Navajo Area had the most deaths with 7.

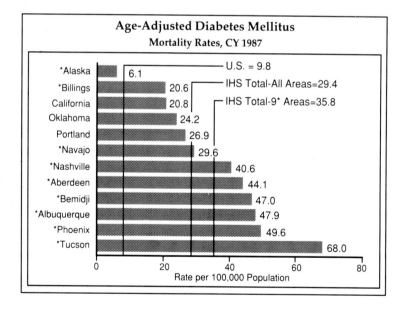

Age-Adjusted Diabetes Mellitus
Mortality Rates, CY 1987

- U.S. = 9.8
- IHS Total-All Areas=29.4
- IHS Total-9* Areas=35.8

Area	Rate
*Alaska	6.1
*Billings	20.6
California	20.8
Oklahoma	24.2
Portland	26.9
*Navajo	29.6
*Nashville	40.6
*Aberdeen	44.1
*Bemidji	47.0
*Albuquerque	47.9
*Phoenix	49.6
*Tucson	68.0

Rate per 100,000 Population

In 1987, the age-adjusted diabetes mortality rate for the IHS service area population was 29.4. When the 3 IHS Areas with apparent problems in underreporting of Indian race on death certificates are excluded, the rate is 35.8. This is 265 percent higher than the U.S. All Races rate of 9.8. All of the IHS Area rates were greater than the U.S. rate with the exception of the Alaska rate.

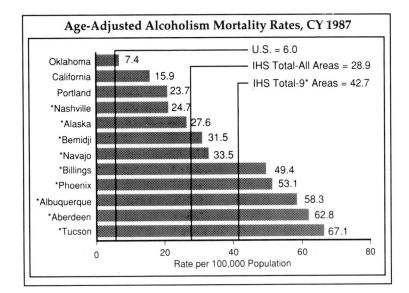

Age-Adjusted Alcoholism Mortality Rates, CY 1987

	Rate per 100,000 Population
Oklahoma	7.4
California	15.9
Portland	23.7
*Nashville	24.7
*Alaska	27.6
*Bemidji	31.5
*Navajo	33.5
*Billings	49.4
*Phoenix	53.1
*Albuquerque	58.3
*Aberdeen	62.8
*Tucson	67.1

U.S. = 6.0
IHS Total-All Areas = 28.9
IHS Total-9* Areas = 42.7

In 1987, the age-adjusted alcoholism mortality rate for the IHS service area population was 28.9. When the 3 IHS Areas with apparent problems in underreporting of Indian race on death certificates are excluded, the rate is 42.7. This is 612 percent higher than the U.S. All Races rate of 6.0. The Tuson Area rate of 67.1 was over 11 times the U.S. rate.

Age-Adjusted Alcoholism Mortality Rates
Calendar Year 1987

	Deaths	Rate [1]
U.S. All Races	15,909	6.0
All IHS Areas	217	28.9
9 * Areas [2]	178	42.7
Aberdeen *	29	62.8
Alaska *	15	27.6
Albuquerque *	15	58.3
Bemidji *	10	31.5
Billings *	14	49.4
California	10	15.9
Nashville *	7	24.7
Navajo *	39	33.5
Oklahoma	12	7.4
Phoenix *	35	53.1
Portland	17	23.7
Tucson *	8	67.1

[1] Age-adjusted rate per 100,000 population.
Rates based on a small number of deaths should be interpreted with caution.
[2] The 3 IHS Areas that do not have an asterisk (California, Oklahoma, and Portland) appear to have a problem with underreporting of Indian race on death certificates. Therefore a separate IHS rate was calculated excluding these 3 Areas.

Education

Student performance and participation is far below the national average -

- 52% finish high school.

- 17% attend college.

- 4% graduate from college.

- 2% attend graduate school.

Why Native Peoples Are At Risk

"Our schools have failed to nurture the intellectual development and academic performance of many native children, as is evident from their high dropout rates and negative attitudes toward school.

Our schools have discouraged the use of Native languages in the classroom, thereby contributing to a weakening of the Natives' resolve to retain and continue the development of their original languages and cultures.

Indian lands and resources are constantly besieged by outside forces interested in further reducing their original holdings.

Political relationships between the tribes and the federal government fluctuate with the will of this U.S. Congress and decisions by the courts."

Excerpt from U.S. Department of Education "Indian Nations At Risk Task Force" - 1991

Economic Welfare

Indians are disadvantaged in the development of business acumen as entrepreneurs. The disparity between the income of Indians and mainstream economics is widening in direct proportion to their lack of experience, opportunity and resources. From a historical perspective, Indians are recent arrivals to the political and economic arena.

- 75% of the work force earn less than $7,000 per year.

- 45% are below the poverty level.

- The average unemployment rate is 45%.

- Unemployment on some reservations is 90%.

Most housing is inadequate and substandard. For instance, Navajos who have the largest reservation and tribe with the most resources endure the following conditions:

- 46% have no electricity.

- 54% have no indoor plumbing.

- 82% live without a telephone.

These Third World living conditions are typical of most reservation communities. Poor health care, miserable poverty and substandard education are a daily fact of life for most American Indians.

"An objective evaluation of the Indian condition would conclude that systems and programs employed for the last 100 years are not working very well."

Gaming is the current economic and political issue in Indian country.

The issue of Indian sovereignty hangs in the balance as Indians cautiously negotiate the maze of overlapping state and federal jurisdictions and control.

Casinos seem to be a quick-fix basis for cash flow - a short term solution for long-term problems. It is very difficult to argue with success, however, the jury is still out on the long-term ramifications of gaming on Indian social and economic development.

Some of the Indian casinos are generating fantastic revenues. Some tribes with smaller enrollment are distributing per capita payments. Theoretically and literally, tribal members have become millionaires in a very short period of time.

This brings up a number of issues: Does this wealth translate into shared wealth with alienated tribal members and their Urban Indian counterparts? What will be the attitude of the federal government and the public toward subsidy programs as the tribal coffers fill? Will there still be health, education and welfare subsidy programs for tribal members who are considered millionaires?

What will be the attitude and reaction of adjacent non-Indian communities toward the Indian gaming bonanza? Will there be a saturation of the gaming market with a casino on every corner? Or will there be a backlash as casino money machines absorb too much discretionary income?

Divide aNd CoNquer

The federal government spends over $3 billion annually on Indian programs. Estimates indicate that ten cents of every dollar actually reaches those desperately in need. Every year or so Congress produces a report and/or an investigation. The sad truth is that little if any meaningful reform reaches the grassroots level.

Indians initiate sporadic uprisings which receive brief notoriety and media exposure. However, as public and political attention wanes, it is business as usual. An objective evaluation of the Indian condition would conclude that systems and programs employed for the last 100 years are not working very well.

The most effective strategy to incapacitate and destroy any organization is by internal division. Indians are particularly vulnerable to this strategy because of egocentric tribalism. They have been divided historically by circumstance and design.

Indian issues are mired in a morass of demographics complicated by tribalism:

- Nearly 2 million self-declared Indians.

- Approximately 1.2 million Indians enrolled.

- 319 federally recognized tribes.

- 250 different languages and dialects.

- 308 federally recognized reservations.

• 30+ state recognized reservations.

The monumental task of administration and management of this demographic nightmare has been the responsibility of the BIA. The BIA has been the subject of severe criticism in the execution of its responsibilities on behalf of Indians. There is a current movement to restructure or abolish the BIA and allow the tribes to govern themselves through self-determination.

SUMMARY

Indians are a durable and resourceful people. They have survived 400 years of genocide and 100 years of BIA dominance and government control. They have a strong spirituality closely tied to the land and their religions reflect a respect for the mysterious powers of nature.

For the moment, it appears that the pendulum of social conscience has swung in favor of the Indians. People of conscience are empathetic to the plight of Indians. In the academic community there are concerted efforts to include a more accurate account of American Indian history and culture.

Empathy is wonderful, however, **Indians must take control of their own destiny.** Historically, when political and economic forces covet Indian land and resources, social conscience is compromised. Avarice has the inherent ability to justify and rationalize it's actions. The same ends can now be accomplished through clever paper and political manipulations rather than physical aggression of the past.

The idea that native people can live in tranquil harmony with nature on reservations is an illusion.

> **"The BIA has been the subject of severe criticism in the execution of its responsibilities on behalf of the Indians."**

Today's Indians cannot walk the path their ancestors walked. The last bargaining chip are the reservations and the respective resources. Indians must take appropriate precautions to protect those remaining resources.

2090

For thousands of years, tribalism was an instinct that was necessary for survival. Tribalism has an upside and a downside. The upside is that tribalism is a source of Indian strength, culture and tradition. The downside is that tribalism has been at the heart of Indian dissension since Plymouth Rock.

Egocentric tribalism is not conducive to the development of significant national political or economic power. Democracy is a game of numbers and the majority rules. Of the 2 million self-declared Indians in the country, approximately 1.2 million are enrolled. The enrolled Indian population is less than 1/2 of 1% of the total population of 258 million!

- It is questionable what percentage of the enrolled Indian population participates in the political process that controls every aspect of their lives.

- Nearly all reservation lands are held in "trust" by the federal government. **The Congressional fox is guarding the Indian chicken coop.**

- 11 million acres (20%) within reservation boundaries are owned by non-Indians.

"During 1992, we will honor this country's native peoples as vital participants in the history of the United States. This year gives us the opportunity to recognize the special place that Native Americans hold in our society, to affirm the right of Indian tribes to exist as sovereign entities, and to seek greater mutual understanding and trust.""

President George Bush - March 1992

- Nearly one-half (46%) of the reservation population are non-Indians.

- Less than 10% of contemporary Indians speak their native language.

- Indians continue to be a political embarrassment and an economic thorn in the side of federal and state governments.

➤ CHAPTER 4 • A Plan of Action

Indian Image

Indians have always had a public relations problem because they did not have the means to tell their story. They became the hapless victims of a one-sided relentless media campaign that created stereotypical images primarily for entertainment.

Spearheaded by western pulp novels and the movies, Indians became a monosyllable drunken savage, living in teepees, usually in a feathered headdress with warpaint, dancing and whooping around a fire. The character assassination was complete to the last detail. America embraced the fictional image to the extent that new myths were based on old myths.

As a result, the Indian has been relegated to the past, the villainous savage of John Wayne movies, comedic trivialization, or worse, as sports teams and their mascots. Time and attrition have desensitized America and provided immunization to the real pain and tragedy of today's American Indians.

Psychologically, a less-than-human Indian image was necessary to sanction conquest and to soothe the nation's moral conscience. The best image Indians could hope for was as a Tonto or Little Beaver as trusted companions to their superior white counterparts.

America's conscience has been appeased with regard to the Indian condition by misinformation, disinformation and complacency. Contemporary American Indians have become invisible in the mind's eye of the nations's conscience. When there is reference to minorities, the focus is on African-Americans, Hispanics, Asians and "others." American Indians are included among the "others."

> **"For a subject worked and reworked so often in novels, motion pictures and television, American Indians remain probably the least understood and most misunderstood Americans of us all."**
>
> **President John F. Kennedy, 1963**

Indians must shoulder their share of responsibility for conduct which has contributed to their negative image. It is the responsibility of the Indian community to replace that negative image with a more accurate and positive image - a renaissance Indian.

Indians have contributed immensely to the plagiarism of certain culture, traditions and ceremonies by public display at pow wows. The public is invited and are coyly asked not to take pictures of certain sacred ceremonies. Perhaps there should be public pow wows and private pow wows. Each with its own agenda and purpose.

Can we realistically expect today's society to be compassionate about Indian problems? Today's society is oblivious to memories of the Great Depression and World War II, and has only fading memories of Vietnam and civil rights marches. They are certainly not concerned with atrocities perpetrated generations before they were born.

There are literally hundreds of programs, agencies, organizations and publications that are concerned with Indian issues. The effective entities must develop a centralized communication system that nurtures interaction and networking. Computer networks such as IndianNet, NativeNet, AisesNet, et al, have provided a window of opportunity to establish a national Indian communications network.

> "Computer networks such as IndianNet, NativeNet, AisesNet, et al, have provided a window of opportunity to establish a national Indian communications network."

A Ten-Year Agenda

Indians cannot rely on the benevolence of the United States government. Government subsidies for necessities of life are not the answer to Indian future. The answers are education, political unity and economic independence.

Indian destiny is at a crossroads and the moment for effective action is at hand. An agenda can be developed which will result in a healing process for the country and **all** Indians. Indians can take control of their destiny by a realistic ten-year plan.

Indians are a privileged people who want exclusivity. Indians are a special people, but they cannot be a separate people.

There is nothing is as sure as change and adaptability is an absolute for survival. To meet the challenges of the future, American Indians must develop a three-level agenda:

Individually

- Education, education, education...

- Get actively involved politically. Register and vote on your 21st birthday.

- Develop a positive physical image which includes confronting alcoholism and obesity. (Quit drinking booze as a way of life and eating frybread as a daily staple.)

- Nurture unique spirituality.

- Maintain cultural affiliation.

Tribally

- Focus on national American Indian identity first and tribal affiliation second. Indians are one race of people with 319 tribes - not 319 different races.

- Cast aside archaic tribal animosities and prejudices that often date back hundreds of years. They smack of racism.

- Establish progressive and definitive enrollment requirements. These requirements could include several status classifications with commensurate entitlements and responsibilities.

Who is and who isn't "Indian" must be redefined

"Indians and their leaders must be prepared to re-examine conventional wisdom... If there is one lesson of the last decade, it is that creativity and originality combined with well based historical and legal research provides the ammunition to force a re-evaluation of Indian law and policy."

Citizenship &
American Indians
Helen Burgess - 1990

by current criteria that will result in a rational and equitable solution. Insidious forces are at work that are dividing Indians by various categories. The end result is that there are not enough people in any one category to be politically or economically significant.

- Aggressively solicit and expand tribal enrollment. Include everyone who meets tribal enrollment qualifications by issuance of a picture enrollment card. There are 10 to 15 million at-large potential Indian votes! Indian traditionalist must realize that in order to survive, they must embrace their urban brethren. It is not prudent for any group to exclude the largest segment (80%) of its constituency.

- Orchestrate a united tribal voting political coalition on the major Indian issues of health, education and welfare.

   Establish a strategic geographic political agenda. In certain political arenas, a united Indian vote could be the deciding factor in important elections and issues. Every aspect of Indian life is determined by fickle political decisions. Indians live a precarious and fragile political existence.

Nationally

- Develop a militant strategy campaign to marshal participants and resources. Analyze strengths and weaknesses.

- Initiate a national public relations campaign to penetrate the nation's conscience — a sustained multi-faceted professional campaign.

- Utilize the above public relations campaign to solicit global community opinion and support by exploitation and exposure of the Indian condition.

- Establish specific national concessions as retribution for past grievances.

- Establish national political unity to ensure those concessions are mandated.

- Develop a national coalition based on economic enterprise networking.

- Capitalize on the gaming window of opportunity to establish a basis for long-term social and economic development.

  The casinos should contribute a percentage to urban centers for the general welfare and education of Indians.

- Get involved in the Indian computer networks such as IndianNet, NativeNet, AisesNet, et al.

In Conclusion

> *"It seems a basic requirement to study the history of our Indian people. America has much to learn about the heritage of our American Indians. Only though this study can we as a nation do what must be done if our treatment of the American Indian is not to be marked down for all time as a national disgrace."*
>
> **John F. Kennedy - 1963**

Indians are a small but select minority who have the unique feature of millennial ties to this land. They are survivors with a common bond who have withstood 400 years of extermination, termination, assimilation, and other 'ations.' Indians have terminator tenacity. Through all the trials and tribulations, they have sustained a sense of humor. Indians have lost some decisive battles, but not the war.

Immigrants of all races come to this country with a worn suitcase and a dream, 10 years later they are educated and prosperous. Are Indians any less capable? Indians have the responsibility, to those ancestors who fired arrows against cannons and survived against overwhelming odds, to make that survival meaningful.

Indians have had time and opportunity to help correct the course of their own destiny. Indians need to divorce themselves from the helpless victim mindset that blames others for their station in life. The time has come for Indians to help themselves. All that life owes any of us is opportunity, and no one ever said that life was going to be fair.

Public empathy will diminish from this time forward. Too much time has passed and there are too many contemporary issues that have a higher priority. The present generation does not share the social conscience nor will they assume the sins of their forefathers.

Indians must prepare by education to <u>take</u> control of their destiny, as gently as possible. The next battles will be won by warriors whose weapons are the briefcase and computer. The best revenge is to adapt and learn to use the system, to play the game and live well.

America must come to terms with the condition and unresolved issues of American Indians or questions will continue to haunt the nation's conscience. If the Indians lose ... we all lose. Hopefully, the **Digest** has raised more questions than it has answered.

American Indian issues are controversial and complex. We invite constructive criticism, comment and contemporary data. This type of dialogue will improve the composition of future **Digest** editions.

"The next battles will be won by warriors whose weapons are the briefcase and computer."

➤ BIBLIOGRAPHY

MATERIAL REFERENCE LIST

This list contains the names and phone numbers of reference material sources so that the reader may explore the respective Indian issues in depth. Most of these publications are free.

1. **We The First Americans**
   Racial Statistics Branch
   Population Division
   Bureau of the Census
   Washington DC 20233
   (301)763-4100
   Issued September 1993, this 17 page booklet is a comprehensive profile of Indian demographics. It is well written and compiled by experts.

2. **1992 Statistical Abstract**
   Teaching Supplement for Grades 5-12
   Bureau of the Census
   (301)763-1510 - Education Program
   Order a 28 page catalog "Statistics Aren't Static."
   The catalog contains a synopsis of the 1992 Statistical Abstract and order forms. The Census Bureau is very helpful and a wealth of information.

3. **American Indian & Alaska Native Areas: 1990**
   Bureau of the Census - published June 1991
   Racial Statistics Branch Population Division
   (301)763-4040
   The 52 page report list all recognized Indian reservations in alphabetical order showing aggregate and Indian population of each reservation. It also provides some insight and parameters for the methods of census taking.

4. **Indian Labor Force**
   Bureau of Labor Statistics - January 1991
   Public Affairs Office
   (202)208-3711
   The purpose of the 32 page report is to identify and determine the status of the

Indian labor force living on Federal reservations or in areas or communities adjacent to reservations. The report is mostly demographic tables.

5. **Federal Register of Recognized Tribes**
BIA Tribal Services - October 1993
(202)208-7445
The Federal Register is a 7 page list of all Federally recognized tribes in alphabetical order that is updated periodically.

6. **Tribal Leaders Directory**
BIA - Division of Tribal Government Services
Office of Public Information - January 1992
(202)208-3710
The 67 page directory lists all tribal leaders, addresses and telephone numbers. The information is listed by Area Offices in alphabetical order.

7. **List of Tribal Petitioners**
BIA Branch of Acknowledgment & Research - March 1993
(202)208-3592
The 24 page report is a list of the tribes petitioning for recognition. The report includes names, addresses, telephone numbers and dates of petition. The information is listed in alphabetical order by states.

8. **Annual Report of Indian Lands**
BIA Office of Trust Responsibilities
Real Estate Department - September 1985
(202)208-7737
The 107 page report should only be ordered if you are interested in extensive detail. The numbers can get very confusing. The information is listed by Area Office in alphabetical order. There are problems in the agency department because the last "annual" report is dated September 1985.

9. **Indian Land Areas**
U.S. Geological Survey - Revised 1992
In Cooperation with the BIA & Smithsonian Institute.
The 26" x 42" folded map is in color and has been the standard when it is available.

10. **Regional Differences in Indian Health 1993**
Indian Health Service
Office of Planning, Evaluation, and Legislation
Division of Program Statistics

Parklawn Building, Room 6-41
5600 Fishers Lane
Rockville MD 20857
(301)443-1180
The 86 page report is mostly demographic tables preceded by 11 pages of explanatory text that present a comprehensive overview of Indian health and the structure of the Indian Health Service facilities. Other reports are available.

11. **American Indians Today**
BIA Public Information Office - 1991
(202)208-3711
The 36 page booklet answers many basic questions with regard to American Indians by using a question and answer format. The booklet has an extensive list of "Where to Find More Information About Indians" and a good bibliography.

12. **Indian Nations At Risk**
U.S. Department of Education
Indian Nations At Risk Task Force - 1992
(202)708-5366
The sub-title is "An Educational Strategy for Action". The 60 page booklet is very well done and easy to read.

13. **Atlas of Native History**
Jack D. Forbes - 1981
University of California
Native American Studies
Davis, CA 95616-8667
(916)752-3237
The 8 page newspaper format is a definitive study of the migrations of Indian tribes beginning in the 1500s illustrated by a series of maps. A unique feature is the Indian version of tribal names referenced to the English version of the same name.

14. **Histories & Statistical Information on Oklahoma's Resident Tribes & Nations.**
Oklahoma Indian Affairs Commission
4545 N. Lincoln, Suit 282
Oklahoma City, OK 73105
(405)521-3828
The 15 page report is a roster of Indian tribes in Oklahoma. Because the large concentration of tribes relocated to Oklahoma came from a wide range of geographic areas, each tribal synopsis presents a much larger view of Indian America than is indicated by the geographic area.

15. **Citizenship & American Indians**
    by Helen Burgess
    (Same address as above.)
    The 5 page dissertation is insightful and thought provoking with regard to Indian political history and orientation.

Catalogs of Indian Publications

There are a multitude of excellent publications available that cover every aspect of Indianology. Rather than provide an abbreviated list which would exclude some great reading, We have listed a few organizations that have catalogs with extensive inventories that are available for the asking.

1. **American Indian Science & Engineering Society**
   1630 30th Street, Suite 301
   Boulder, CO 80301
   Catalog of Merchandise
   (303)492-8658

2. **Four Winds Trading Company**
   685 South Broadway, Suite A
   Boulder, CO 80303
   (800)456-5444

3. **Native American Public Broadcasting Consortium, Inc.**
   PO Box 83111
   Lincoln, NE 68501
   (402)472-3522

4. **Maverick Distributors**
   Drawer 7289
   Bend, OR 97708
   (800)333-8046

5. **Written Heritage**
   8009 Wales Street
   New Orleans, LA 70126
   (504)246-3742

6. **Smithsonian Institution Press**
   Department 900
   Blue Ridge
   Summit, PA 17294-0900

Genealogy has become the nation's No. 3 hobby behind coin and stamp collecting. Establishing one's ethnic background can be rewarding, satisfying, and sometimes quite surprising! Verification of ancestry precipitates a sense continuity, knowledge and perspective. However, the process can be time-consuming and frustrating.

Indian Genealogy research can be especially frustrating, because most Indian tribes did not keep written records. Genealogy identification problems were compounded, when Indian names were replaced by surnames that were easier for the dominant culture to pronounce. Genealogy issues were further complicated by the inter-tribal quandary created during the tribal relocation process.

A successful enrollment campaign will result in a tribal enrollment number and a certification by the respective BIA Area Office. The certification may not entitle the applicant to be enrolled, but it will establish decendency.

How can a person research their Indian ancestry and possibly become tribally enrolled?

- The first step is to research your family genealogy. Talk to older relatives and check family records, documents, bibles, wills and other sources of family history.

- The Church of the Jesus Christ of Latter-day Saints (Mormons) have the best genealogy resources in the world. They hold Indians in high regard and give special attention to Indian genealogy. Each church is affiliated with a Family History Center that is connected by a computer network to all other resource centers. The staff will help you do the research or they will do the research for a nominal fee.

- Most libraries have genealogy sections and some with Indian resources.

- Libraries have listings and can refer you to numerous government agencies and Indian organizations.

- Contact your respective tribal enrollment officer for tribal enrollment requirements, application forms and direction.

- A BIA booklet "American Indians Today" lists several national resources. (Booklet referenced on page 59.)

- There are a number of private and non-profit genealogy organizations with extensive resources.

- Computer resources and national bulletin board networks are available.

BIA Area Offices

(#)-Denotes the number of tribes including their component entities.

DEPARTMENT OF THE INTERIOR

BUREAU OF INDIAN AFFAIRS
1849 C STREET, N.W.
WASHINGTON, DC 20240
(202) 208-3711

ABERDEEN AREA OFFICE
NE, ND, SD-(16)
115 4th Avenue, S.E.
Aberdeen, SD 57401-4382
(605) 226-7343

MINNEAPOLIS AREA OFFICE
IA, MI, MN, WI-(31)
331 Second Avenue South
Minneapolis, MN 55401-2241
(612) 373-1000

ALBUQUERQUE AREA OFFICE
CO, NM-(25)
615 First Street, N.W.
Albuquerque, NM 87125-6567
(505) 766-3171

MUSKOGEE AREA OFFICE
OK-(18)
Old Federal Building
101 N. 5th Street
Muskogee, OK 74401-6206
(918) 687-2296

ANADARKO AREA OFFICE
KS, OK-(24)
WCD Office Complex
P.O. Box 368
Anadarko, OK 73005-0368
(405) 247-6673

NAVAJO AREA OFFICE
AZ, NM, UT-(4)
P.O. Box 1060
Gallup, NM 87305
(505) 863-8315

BILLINGS AREA OFFICE
MT, WY-(8)
316 North 26th Street
Billings, MT 59101-1397
(406) 657-6315

PHOENIX AREA OFFICE
AZ, ID, NV, UT-(50)
1 North First Street
P.O. Box 10
Phoenix, AZ 85001-0010
(602) 379-6600

EASTERN AREA OFFICE
NY, ME, LA, FL, NC,
MS, CT, RI-(22)
3701 North Fairfax Dr., #260
Arlington, VA 22203
(703) 235-2571

PORTLAND AREA OFFICE
OR, WA, ID-(42)
911 NE 11th Avenue
Portland, OR 97232-4169
(503) 231-6702

JUNEAU AREA OFFICE
AK-(220)
Federal Building
P.O. Box 3-8000
Juneau, AK 99802-1219
(907) 586-7177

SACRAMENTO AREA OFFICE
CA-(90)
Federal Building
2800 Cottage Way
Sacramento, CA 95825-1884
(916) 978-4691

In order to understand the current problems and issues of American Indians, it is essential to know the answers to the basic questions: *What is the size and location of today's Indian population, tribes and reservations?* These two maps provide a national frame of reference to help answer these questions. Both maps are 24" x 36", full-color, shaded relief and laminated. These easy-to-read wall maps are an ideal reference for schools, libraries, government agencies, gaming industry or anyone interested in American Indians.

ISBN 1-881933-01-6 $15.00

The map of **American Indian History** is a historical synopsis of Indian America.

- Graphics of dimished land base as Indians were forced westward by encroaching settelers.

- Location of 308 federally recognized reservations.

- Location and dates of major Indian battles.

- Location of major forts and dates of activity.

The map of **American Indian Nations** is a visual composite of contemporary demographics.

- BIA Area Office administrative boundaries.

- Location of over 308 federally recognized reservations.

- The roster lists the size in acres and the population of each reservation.

- Reservations with gaming facilities are indicated.

ISBN 1-881933-01-4 $15.00

Buy these maps at your local retail outlet, it will save you time and shipping costs. If they are not available, call Thunderbird Enterprises at 1 (800) 835-7220